HOW CATERING SUCKED THE LIFE RIGHT OUT OF ME

....

SUDI "RICK" KARATAS

Sudirick Publishing
VAN NUYS, CALIFORNIA

Disclaimer: All the stories in the book are true, although some of the names and identifying details of the people mentioned in the book have been changed to protect their privacy.

Sudirick Books / Sudi "Rick" Karatas
www.sudirick.com
sudirick@aol.com

Copy editing by Stephanie Gunning
Cover design by Sudi "Rick" Karatas and Rebecacovers
Book Layout © Book Design Templates

How Catering Sucked the Life Right Out of Me / Sudi "Rick" Karatas. —1st ed.

Library of Congress Control Number 2020921097

ISBN 978-1-7359043-0-6 (paperback)
ISBN 978-1-7359043-1-3 (kindle ebook)
ISBN 978-1-7359043-2-0 (epub ebook)

To my family, including my mom, Terry, one of the best cooks ever, my late dad, Nevzat, my brothers and sisters, Sibel, Suzie, Kenan, and Kevin, and all my relatives in Upstate New York and in Turkey, and my partner, Carlos Romani.

Contents

Preface		1
Chapter 1	The Pros of Doing Catering	3
Chapter 2	Don't Bite the Hand That Feeds You	5
Chapter 3	Early Beginnings	19
Chapter 4	Brushes with Celebrities	27
Chapter 5	Catering 101: Cocktail Hour and the Grueling Hours That Follow	47
Chapter 6	Pet Peeves: Annoying Things Guests Do	59
Chapter 7	Nightmares *Not* on Elm Street	71
Chapter 8	How Do You (Dis) Like Them Bad Apples?	81
Chapter 9	More Rotten Apples in the Catering Orchard	103
Chapter 10	Weddings, Bar Mitzvahs, and Birthdays, Oh My!	113
Chapter 11	The Good Companies	121
Chapter 12	Eventful Events	141
Chapter 13	Flustercucks: (Horror Stories from Friends and Coworkers	153
Chapter 14	There Are No Holidays for Caterers	167
Chapter 15	Talented People I've Worked With	173
Chapter 16	Ideas I Got While Catering	197
Chapter 17	In Memoriam: Those No Longer with Us	209
Chapter 18	Miscellaneous Mishaps and Catering Chaos	219
Chapter 19	Other Cool and Crazy People I've Worked with: Other Locations	229
Chapter 20	Respect for Caterers	241
Acknowledgments		257
Resources		259
About the Author		261

PREFACE

If you've ever done catering or been to a catered event, this book is for you!

This book is not to discourage ANYONE from doing catering. It is to discourage EVERYONE from doing catering.

In all seriousness (don't expect too much of that), I've actually had a lot of nice experiences catering and met some wonderful people. However, sometimes the bad outweighed the good, so this book is called *How Catering Sucked the Life Right Out of Me.* I'll focus more on the negative experiences because those are the juicier, more entertaining stories!

People love to read about miserable experiences. Suffering and pain is always more interesting than reading about happy campers. Campers who get attacked by bears get much more attention from the press.

I'll dish out some advice and let you in on dozens of secrets about the catering world. I will speak about the truly horrible catering companies and the ones that I enjoyed working for.

This book may encourage you to leave your job if you don't like it or may make you more appreciative of your job, or it may just make you hungry.

I'll give you lots of food for thought—literally. Hopefully, it will make you laugh, cry, teach you what not to do at catering events, and it definitely will make you crave the mini hot dogs!

(I've got a) *bon* (to pick) *appetit.*

Sudi "Rick" Karatas

ONE

THE PROS OF DOING CATERING

TWO

DON'T BITE THE HAND THAT FEEDS YOU

Okay. Just trying to be funny in chapter 1, implying there are no pros. They say, "Don't bite the hand that feeds you," so I will admit there are some good things about catering. For example, they did feed us. Most companies anyway. But sometimes it wasn't until seven hours into a shift.

A few caterers didn't feed us at all. One New York caterer didn't feed his staff but told us, "A smart waiter never goes hungry," meaning "Sneak food discretely every chance you get."

One of the first catering jobs I did in California, I arrived at an event and found out we wouldn't be getting a break to eat for at least seven hours. I was already hungry when I got there. It ticked me off that they were going to make us wait that long, so before the event started and after everything was set up, I quickly ducked out. I snuck downstairs to my car in the parking lot and drove a few blocks to a Carl's Jr. I would have gone to an In-N-Out Burger but it's more like In-Wait-a-Little-While-Out Burger because there is usually a long line, and I was in a hurry. When I got back, I rushed back upstairs with the bag of food and back onto the floor. I had returned within twenty minutes.

The guy in charge saw me coming in with the bag of food and asked me if I'd left the event to go get the food. I said, "Of course not, I just went to my car to get it." I told him it was leftovers from earlier and I needed a little solid food in order to take medication and I could NOT wait seven hours to have something in my stomach. Yes, I lied. Sue me! But hey, screw them for starving us!

He bought it, I guess, seemed relieved, and said, "Oh good, because you should never abandon an event."

The way he said *abandon* made it seem like I was abandoning a child. Meanwhile I didn't miss anything from the event, the guests were not even there yet.

The Pros and Perks of Doing Catering

Now I will tell you about the few positives about doing catering.

Flexibility. Catering is the perfect job for struggling actors, musicians, and students because of the flexibility. If you need to cancel a shift for an audition the next day, you can. If you book commercial or film work for the next day, they can often get someone to cover for you. If you need to take a month off and go shoot a film, you can, and then come back. You can't do this if you have a nine to five job.

Free food. Yes, you get free food. You can be an out of work actor, but you don't have to be a STARVING out of work actor. (A con could be that you gain weight from all the fattening food around you, so this really cancels out the pro.) You can even sometimes bring free food home. Most caterers don't let you, yet they throw it out right in front of you, so screw 'em and fill those Ziplock bags you brought with you. I hate to see food wasted like that when people are starving . . . in my apartment!

Free concerts/shows/entertainment. At many of the events, there are performances by big entertainers that servers watch for free. Actually, we get paid to enjoy a show. I've seen many and will talk about them shortly.

Being in really nice houses. I've been in many fancy homes with views overlooking Manhattan or all of L.A.. When I worked in these houses, I would say to myself, *Wow, look at all they have! What am I doing wrong?* Then I would think, *No wait! What are THEY doing wrong?* Because to make that much money they had to be doing something wrong, right?

Off the books. Some of the jobs are cash, off the books. Hopefully, no one from the IRS is reading this. Of course, I reported all of my earnings and tips (in case the IRS is reading this), but perhaps some people don't. <Wink>

The pay. Is not horrible. The rate is usually between $20 and $35 an hour, sometimes a little more. And sometimes there is a tip of anywhere from $20–$100 (from the catering companies who don't steal or keep the tips.)

Coworkers. You get to work with many cool, creative people because most are actors, musicians, or artists. (Many are crazy who are in those fields, so this may also negate the pro.) Seriously, I have developed lifelong friendships. You also work with so many different people, whereas in a restaurant it's mostly the same small group every day.

It's not monotonous. Since you're not always at the same place or the same type of party, it's more interesting than if you work in a hotel, restaurant, or club. There is a lot of variety. Some people don't like that as they prefer stability and the same schedule.

No taking menu orders. These events usually have either a buffet or one main course. Once in a while, there is a choice of two things they can order, but it's not like a restaurant where, as a server, you have to memorize the menu and say what today's specials are (which are really yesterday's leftovers).

No dealing with cash. Usually, that is the case. There is no cash register. Once in a while, there is a cash bar for bartenders. So, no adding or writing up a bill, bringing a check, making change, or swiping a credit card.

Clearly, there are quite a few positive things about catering although not enough to fill up a whole chapter, so now back to discussing the negative things:

I'm kidding. Here are some more positives things.

Free Concerts

Getting Physical

Catering can be very **physical.** (You'll see what I did there in a minute.) One of the best perks of doing these jobs is that we often see many famous people perform or do concerts, sometimes even warm up and rehearse. I was setting up a ballroom at one of the venues in the early 2000s, putting silverware on the tables with the rest of the butlers, and we could hear a band warming up. A woman started to sing the song "Physical" and I said, "Wow! She really sounds a lot like Olivia Newton-John." Then I turned around to see one of my all-time favorites singing onstage in jeans and tee-shirt: Miss Olivia Newton-John!

I honestly love her. I was in heaven and was getting paid to see Olivia rehearse! Turns out it was an Australia Week celebration and she was the entertainment.

She rehearsed a few songs and sounded great. Later, I snuck in the room while she performed for the guests. Technically, we were not supposed to be on the floor at that time. But I won't say anything (if you don't).

I later worked another fundraiser where she sang a few songs along with Sheryl Crow on a huge tennis court at someone's house. I have never met her, but I listen to her music all the time.

House Concert with Johnny Mathis

When I was younger and in my mid-twenties, many people told me I looked like Johnny Mathis. He was in his fifties, and of course, is black, which I am not but I was very, very tan from my lifeguarding job and my sun-worshipping lifestyle. Back then, I was drawn to beach life and sun like a moth to a flame. Ironically, since living in California, I actually spend a lot less time in the sun than I did when I lived on the East Coast.

Where was I? Oh yes, Johnny Mathis. "Chances Are" I will go off on many more tangents throughout this book. (See what I did there?) Anyway, the parents of Rich Hance, one of my best friends, told me for years I looked like Johnny Mathis. Wish I could sing like him. Then I wouldn't have had to do catering and you wouldn't have the pleasure of reading this book.

So, cut to twenty years later and I'm working a house party for a woman's sixtieth birthday party and they hired Johnny Mathis to sing for the party. He was probably in his late sixties at this point, put on a great show, and sounded "Wonderful, Wonderful." (See what I did there again?) On his way up to the stage to perform, he walked right past me.

While still there, I called Rich and said, "Guess who's singing at this house party where I'm working?"

Without missing a beat, he said, "Johnny Mathis."

Missed Dolly Twice

My all-time favorite entertainer, Dolly Parton, sang at two events where a caterer for whom I worked had been booked. This company had me working elsewhere both nights, so I missed both possibilities of seeing her. At one of the events, which was an Oscar party, she sang the Oscar-nominated song called "Travelin' Thru" that she had written for the film *TransAmerica*. I was so mad I missed it. The other party she had attended, along with Lily Tomlin and Jane Fonda, was celebrating the twenty fifth anniversary of *9 to 5.*

My coworker worked in the green room for that and got to meet her. I was so bummed and envious. He didn't even like her. I no longer speak to him, for other reasons.

We don't know what events and performers are booked beforehand. We just show up where we are assigned. Had I known about the ones when Dolly would appear, I would have begged and pleaded to work those gigs. I would have even done it for free. I worship Dolly.

Kenny Loggins

I saw Kenny Loggins sing for an hour and a half at the Event Deck in Los Angeles a few years back. I was paid to stand behind a buffet and listen to a great concert. Kenny wanted me to sing on the Loggins and Messina songs with him since Messina was not there, but I had chicken to serve for the buffet, so I had to pass.

Just kidding. I discretely danced a little behind the buffet, during his performance of "Footloose." Sometimes you gotta cut loose.

Cyndi Lauper

I actually served hors d'oeuvres to Cindi Lauper once and she was very nice. I love her accent. I was able to see her perform for about an hour at another event I worked in Hollywood. She was awesome, but because it was a company party she'd been hired for, not everyone was into it. A few guests were over in a corner not even paying attention.

Seeing this, Cyndi joked, "Go ahead talk amongst yourselves," in her Brooklyn accent. She was very funny and sang her heart out and put on a great show, and most of the guests did enjoy it, as did the staff. After all, servers just wanna have fun too!

Donna Summer, Seal, and David Foster

I worked an event in L.A. that was a fundraiser. At my table sat Bill Clinton and Barbra Streisand. The entertainment was David Foster and friends. Donna Summer sang with Seal. Since Barbra Streisand was at my table, I tried to coax her to go sing her duet with Donna "No More Tears, Enough Is Enough." I mean, c'mon, how many times are you going to have Donna Summer and Barbra Streisand in the same room?

Anyway, she wouldn't budge.

Okay, I didn't really talk to her. Seal sounded great, Donna Summer looked and sounded great. A year and a half later, she died of lung cancer. I was shocked. She was only sixty-three. I read that it resulted from the 9/11 pollution in the air. She lived near that area in Manhattan.

Lady Gaga and the Divine Miss M

I worked a house party where Lady Gaga sang. (This was before the film *A Star Is Born* but after her first two smash CDs). She was singing and halfway through abruptly stopped, looked at the divine Bette Midler sitting at a table, and said, "Oh, hi!" She seemed taken aback and in awe seeing someone of that magnitude in the room.

Other guests included Don Rickles and Bob Newhart, and even Nancy Reagan was wheeled in for the cocktail hour in a wheelchair. This was about six months before she died.

Other Free Performances

I saw quite a few other concerts for free, like:

- Lady Antebellum singing at the Microsoft Theatre for about forty-five minutes. They were really good. This is before they changed their name to Lady A.
- The Beach Boys sang a full set in the Hamptons when the hit "Kokomo" was out.
- The Eagles performed (before Glenn Frey passed) at the Wiltern Theatre in Los Angeles.
- Earth, Wind & Fire performed in Hollywood. They were very good.
- Toni Braxton sang for about an hour at the Microsoft Theater. She was really good.
- Marc Cohen was the guest entertainer at a fundraiser in NYC, about a year or two after winning a Grammy for his song "Walking in Memphis." Many guests just kept talking at their tables during his performance. They were so rude.
- Jon Bon Jovi sang a few songs, just him and a guitar, at a fundraiser. He sang three songs, one of which was "Hallelujah," the Leonard Cohen composition. He did a good job on it.
- Def Leppard sang at the *Rock of Ages* premiere.

- Vince Gill, Zac Brown, Jason Mraz, and Emmylou Harris all sang a few songs in the round at the Microsoft Theater.
- Carole King sang a few songs at a fundraiser.
- Band Perry performed at an outdoor event in downtown L.A..
- James Taylor, Paul Simon, and José Feliciano performed a few songs in the Hamptons.
- Willie Nelson sang at a party I worked in the late 1990s. No, I didn't sing "To All the Girls I've Loved Before" with him.
- Paul Lekakis, sang his hit "Boom Boom (Let's Go Back to My Room)" in the late 1980s at an event I worked for Rick Kleid, owner of a company called Helping Hands, who staffed events. It was a man's thirtieth birthday party where most of the guests were LGBT.

I love music and concerts so being able to see some of these performers while I'm getting paid is one of the few things about catering I could stomach. (How many puns is that in the book so far?) Seeing artists perform for free is my favorite catering perk.

While I saw James Taylor sing just a few songs in the Hamptons, my coworker and friend Tia Roberts has a great catering/James Taylor story.

I was working a charity event when I learned that one of my favorite artists, James Taylor, was performing. I was jumping out of my skin with the hope of meeting him. I saw his manager and told her of my love for him and she invited me to his dressing room. As I entered, she introduced me as "One of his number one fans." She then left the room with just the two of us, me and JT side by side! I couldn't believe it! I expressed the enormity of his music and said that no matter what I say to him it would never convey what he means to me. We spoke a good five minutes, just the two of us. We spoke of songs and concerts past—a true dialog!

As I gathered myself to leave, I looked at him, raised my arm in the air, and with the movement of my hand said, "God, Paul McCartney, You."

He chuckled and said, "How kind." It was the greatest moment in my life up to that moment.

The second greatest moment is when I went to Rome four years later for my birthday specifically to see JT. Afterwards they had a meet-and-greet. When I approached him, he looked as though he knew me. I told him I was there to celebrate my birthday with him and said, "God, Paul McCartney, You." He immediately lit up and said, "Oh my goodness, yes, I remember you!"

This wouldn't have happened in a million years had it not been for catering.

Dolly Parton to me is what James Taylor is to Tia.

Free Stuff

Another big perk is some of the free gifts we get to take home. Sometimes we get to take the centerpieces with flowers. Sometimes we are given a free bottle of wine. I've gotten many CDs, like *Heart's Greatest Hits,* which is awesome, Carly Simon's *Never Been Gone,* which is really good.

Sometimes we got gift bags. In these, I've gotten Thierry Mugler cologne. I also got the book *Yelling It Like It Is* by Maxine, which is hilarious. And I got about a dozen Stella Artois beer glasses.

I got many tee-shirts from events. I still have my tee-shirts from the premieres of *Breaking Bad* and *Entourage* from ten years ago, though they both fit a little tighter now. Also, I got a Nicole Miller vest and an *American Idol* tee-shirt that had so much glitter on it that it ended up everywhere, so I had to discard it—much like many *Idol* singers have been discarded over the years.

How Much Food Can We Waste and Throw Out?

Speaking of discarding things reminds me of food wasted at events. They say, "Don't bite the hand that feeds you," but maybe we should bite the one that throws out the leftover food that could be fed to the homeless. Don't get Glad get MAD at all the food that is put in the trash at catering events. The Glad and Hefty garbage bag companies are making lots of money thanks to all the food that gets thrown out at catered events. Especially since you have to double bag because one bag may not hold all that heavy, wet food.

Most of the time, catering companies don't give their leftovers to homeless shelters. They would rather throw it out than give it to their staffs or someone who is starving. I swear some companies and chefs and captains even take glee in doing this. It's inexcusable, really, throwing all that good food into the garbage—although I don't hear the rat population complaining. Rats will never go hungry.

I hate to see food go to waste. I'd rather it go around my waist.

Seeing how much food that is wasted in catering makes me feel like throwing up, but that would waste more food. Yet, it definitely leaves a bad taste in my mouth (another pun).

Caterers throw out so much food it should be a crime. The amount of extra food that is made for events is mindboggling, with several buffets and endless amounts that end up in the trash. There might be eight or more buffets that they keep full of food till the very end.

All the extra food is almost always thrown out.

Food as the Enemy

I asked my coworkers what their worst catering experience was. My friend Tia Roberts shared this with me:

The worst experience I had in catering was the food. Don't get me wrong. It was delicious free food, but as a food addict, it was a nightmare. Before every shift, I told myself I'd do better. Yet, inevitably, I lost the battle as I was literally walking into my addiction. Whether it was eating hors d'oeuvres while returning to the kitchen and/or dish room, or scarfing down a meal during our ten-minute break, it wreaked havoc on my life. The problem with the latter is my brain didn't know my stomach was full because I ate so fast, thereby I ate more. Once my brain caught up, I was miserable.

Although it also occurred during breakfast and lunch shifts, the greatest damage was dinner. Whether or not I ate beforehand, I ate again at the end of the night. I spent countless shifts eating dinner any time between 9PM to midnight. It didn't end there. I had the soul crushing task of throwing food away on most of my shifts. I used an army of heavy-duty garbage bags to throw literally tons of food away. It was truly unfathomable.

To lessen the guilt of throwing the food away, I would eat in excess because I couldn't bear having the food go to waste, especially that which came from something that lost its life.

Another catalyst for overeating was my comparison. I spent years standing on the periphery, watching other people's lives and careers flourish as I struggled to move forward in my own. In an effort to silence my thoughts around it, I ate. Catering was a double-edged sword because I so desperately wanted out of that environment, yet I needed the job to support myself.

Turns out I didn't need to stay in the industry to survive, I just needed to change my perspective. I've learned so much about myself and those experiences. I learned to value myself, know my worth, and to have self-compassion.

Thank you, Tia, for sharing your story.

THREE

EARLY BEGINNINGS

Let me back track a little to the time before I started catering.

Syosset Bakery

The first job I ever had was at Syosset Bakery in Syosset, Long Island, when I was sixteen and in high school. This wasn't catering but it was food related. I received $3.35 an hour, which was minimum wage in the early 1980s. After school, I did the hard work in the back of the store, while the boss had the women, including Jacki Leigh and Renee Translateur—still good friends—work the register in the front. My job description was to wash tons of baking trays, clean the oven, sweep and mop the gook-covered floor. It got very dirty in this place. (Not as dirty as my mind, but very dirty.) It was a lot of physical work to clean it. When swim season started, I worked there just on weekends, and probably got more of a workout at the bakery than the 200 laps we did at swim practice.

My boss, Fred, did have the radio on, so at least I could listen to music, and he did have a good sense of humor. He would send me next door to Bahnof's Deli, or as he called them, "Bahnof, the thief" because he thought they overcharged. Fred would have me get him Dinkel Acker beer from there. Haven't heard of that beer since then; don't know if it's still around.

One of Fred's expressions was "Work smarter, not harder," but I don't remember ever not working "harder" on that job. I don't think most kids my age would have worked there for as long as I did. In fact, I think most would have quit on the first day.

One perk of that job was bringing home a lot of free bread, rolls, and so on. I was literally the "bread winner" in the family. The bread I brought home each night, we put in the big freezer in the basement. Sometimes I would bring a few sweets or deserts. Everyone wondered why I didn't gain a bunch of weight while working there. When you're working that hard, you don't have time to eat all those high calorie pastries, and since you are surrounded by it constantly you also get a little sick of it. Also, did I mention I was swimming 200 laps a day at high school swim practice?

Pine Hollow Country Club

After the bakery, the next place I worked in the food service industry was at Pine Hollow Country Club in East Norwich, Long Island, during summers while I was going to college. It was a lot of fun. I worked with a lot of cool people, including Chris Purcell and his sister, Patti, Connie Martinez, Steve

Cromwell, Nancy Adams, and a few others I'm still friends with. I worked there as a busboy one year and as a lifeguard the next, which was a lot more fun and came with a tan. Years later, I ended up working on a commercial on the golf course there.

Working the events at the country club was hard work, but we had good times. All the staff had name tags and one of the waiters put "Young Man" on his since that's what the members all called him. There was a member everyone called Cookie, so my two coworkers and still good friends, Christine Varley and Carrie Ochs, put that on their name tags to be cute, and I still sometimes call them Cookie to this day.

There's a line in the movie *Caddyshack* where Ted Knight's character says, "Don't these people have homes?" because they are practically at the country club all the time. It's 2:00 am and the guests are still there. That line is so funny if you have ever worked in a country club. And if you haven't, it's still funny because of the way Ted Knight says it.

We always were happy when the song "Last Dance" by Donna Summer played because that meant the party was ending and very soon we could go home (or out to party). The song "Last Dance" has a special place in my heart.

The Rocky Horror Picture Show

One Friday night after a shift at Pine Hollow Country Club, we all went to see a midnight showing of *The Rocky Horror Picture Show*. One of the workers "borrowed" a wheelchair from one of the members (when I say "borrowed," I mean they took it from a closet without their knowledge or permission) and brought it to the theater. In the movie, as the guy was being chased around in a wheelchair, one of our coworkers rolled down the aisles of the theater in the wheelchair. (Hey, they wanted audience participation!) We threw toast and rice (that we got from the country club kitchen).

It was an interesting experience, one that people still participate in thirty years later.

My Only Restaurant Job

I have really only done catering work and not restaurant work, except for a few months one year. I worked at Spencer's, which was a restaurant on a golf course in Syosset, Long Island. I worked there with some really fun, wacky people, including Mark Kasper with whom I'm still friends thirty years later. I was in my early to mid-twenties at the time. Just before I started there, I took one of those two-week bartending classes that's supposed to turn you into a professional. Before that, I didn't know how to make anything except maybe gin and tonics and screwdrivers. Afterward, I could make many drinks, including Grasshoppers.

Don't ask me now what is in those because I don't think I ever made one.

Another of the drinks we learned how to make was an Old Fashioned, which I was sure no one would ever order. They were not popular in the 1980s. They are a pain to make, crushing up the bitters and adding orange. That cocktail has made a bit of a comeback in recent years.

Anyway, at Spencer's, we had to make people drinks on the lunch shifts. The very first day I worked, someone asked for, you guessed it (or maybe you didn't, but you should have, the foreshadowing in the previous paragraph was there) an Old Fashioned. I sometimes joke that I became as bitter as an Old Fashioned doing catering. I could not believe someone asked for it, but I knew how to make it.

Of course, I had to taste it to make sure it came out right. Took three or four sips for me to be confident in serving it.

One of the reasons I like catering more than restaurant work is the flexibility. If you're an actor and have to go on auditions, it's easier just to get someone to work for you. At a restaurant, it's much harder. One day when I had off at Spencer's, I did extra work on a TV show in New York City, playing a Lebanese terrorist. The show was *Saturday Night with Connie Chung,* for which they did reenactments about actual events. This episode was about the Terry Anderson hostage story in Iran.

The next day I was at Spencer's and our lunch shift was about to begin when I got a call. (Actually, it was probably a beeper message back then, and I probably called back from a pay phone.) It was the production company from the day before and they asked if I could come into the city right away. They wanted to give me a couple lines as the terrorist on the same show. I said, "Of course." Then I told my boss I had to go. I rushed home and then took the train into the city and did the role.

Luckily, lunches were slow at Spencer's, so it wasn't too big a deal that I ducked out. Actors should always put acting first. I've seen too many aspiring actors get sucked into doing catering full time and then they never do what they would have to do to be successful in what they really want to do.

Creative Temps

Shortly after college, I was looking at the want ads in the paper. This was way before the internet, Craig's list, or Google. I found an ad for Creative Temps, a service that would find you all kinds of side jobs, a few of which were catering gigs. Kathy Vlahov was in charge of the catering and product demonstration department. Most of the jobs were at private Long Island country/golf clubs and a few were helping with inventory at certain companies. One job was a knife demonstrator at a Sears in NYC.

Most jobs were pretty easy and fun, but one was at a tennis tournament the day after a huge storm and it was hard to set everything up because of the damage done. The people running the event were so rude to the staff and spoke to us so very badly that one of the other workers asked me, "Why are they being like this?" And I said, "Because they are assholes."

I thought we were alone when I said this, but someone outside the tent we were in must have heard me. The next day I got a call from Creative Temps that the tennis tournament didn't want me to come back, just because I said someone was an asshole. In the words of Rizzo in *Grease* after she insults Sandy behind her back, "Some people are so touchy." Kathy was in disbelief that I had said what I did as I was usually so nice and polite.

I was originally supposed to work there the whole week, but I was relieved not to have to go back there and deal with those people. Creative Temps put me on something else.

Go for the Gold

I started working with Gold Coast Servers, a staffing company whose motto was "Go for the Gold." They later became Premier Party Servers and Model Bartenders (owned by Marc Levine). Gold Coast hired wait staff to work events for different caterers. We were like rentals.

I've always said, "I can't be bought, but I can be rented."

My association with Gold Coast was how I got sucked into catering.

Some people ask if I do the cooking at any of these events. Hell no. I can pretty much just make toast and I do make a mean shish kabob. Most jobs have their own chefs, or if it's a house party, the host makes the food which the wait staff just reheat and serve.

The Singing Waiter

I'm pretty sure that at quite a few companies I worked for I was known as the "Singing Waiter." Singing to myself and sometimes out loud when I work gets me through many events and makes the time go faster. I love singing. Unfortunately, I can only carry a tune if it's not too heavy. That said, I can safely say I sing better than William Hung, Bob Dylan, Yoko Ono, and Roseanne Barr.

Sometimes I make up parodies while I'm catering. For example, if I'm catering on a Monday, I would go around singing to the melody of the Carpenters song "Rainy Days and Mondays" and change the lyric to "Catering on Mondays always gets me down. Passing food around, feeling like a clown, catering on Monday's always gets me down."

Cara McCarty Chavez, with whom I worked with years ago, told me my singing would get her through some of the nightmare shifts. She remembers I would crack her up when I went scootin' by with a tray and sang to the melody of the song "Hot Hot Hot" and instead I was singing "Get high today, get high today, smoking POT POT POT. A dube on a night like this. I just can't resist. Gonna roll, roll, roll . . . all night long we're gonna do a bong."

I gave Weird Al Yankovic a run for his money.

FOUR

BRUSHES WITH CELEBRITIES

When you cater, you come across many celebrities at events, at least in New York and California anyway. I'm going to drop more names in this chapter than all the plates I've dropped in twenty plus years of catering. I'll try not to talk smack about anyone famous. I can't promise I will succeed, but I will try. I will only say bad things about those who deserve it. Most celebs are nice, and I'll share those stories as well, but then again, people want dirt, don't they? So, let's dig. The names have not been changed to not protect the guilty. Okay, some names have been changed to protect me from lawsuits, but many hints are given.

Daryll Hannah Called Me a God!

No, really. OK, yes, that is taken out of context, but so what? It was at a party in a house of a celebrity couple whom I'm not sure I can name, so I will just say he sang "High Flying Adored" in a movie with Madonna and his wife was a *Working Girl.* Anyway, Daryl Hannah (*Splash, Steel Magnolias)* was sitting on a couch and asked me if there were any more of a certain kind of dessert we had been passing around. I said I would check, so I went back to the kitchen, found some, and brought them out to her. She said and I quote, "Oh, thank you so much. You are a god!" So, I can say truthfully say Daryl Hannah called me a god.

Tom Cruise's House

I worked in Tom Cruise's house once. My job was only to attend to a tiny dessert table. That's pretty much the only room I saw. There were many celebrities in this room: Ellen, Jamie Foxx, and Oprah, among others.

This party took place a short while after Tom Cruise had jumped up and down on the couch on the *Oprah* show. Now, here she was in the living room in Tom Cruise's house. There was a couch in the middle of the room and I so badly wanted to go up to Oprah and say, "I know he jumped on your couch, but please don't jump on his couch." But I didn't have the courage.

I would like to think she would have found it funny, but I wasn't willing to take that chance. I figured it might be *Risky Business,* so I said nothing and stayed by the dessert station while none of the celebrities in the room touched them. God forbid they gain an ounce!

Every single person in this room was a huge celebrity, except me. I didn't even see Tom Cruise while I worked there. If I had, maybe I would have told him Oprah jumped on his couch just to stir things up.

Jack LaLanne Wanted *My* Body

I worked an event where exercise and fitness guru legend Jack LaLanne was seated at my table. He was in his early nineties at this point. My only job was to pour wine. As I stood nearby the table, Jack seemed to keep looking at me, then after a little while, he waved me over. I walked over and he said, "You know what your problem is? You're too good looking! You're like a ten."

Taken aback, I joked, "Oh well, I use your juicer. I guess that helps."

Later, when I went around and poured wine, he slipped me a $10 bill, which was nice but unexpected and rarely happens at these kinds of events. The third time around, he put his arm around my shoulder and asked, "So what do you do out here?"

I said acting, and he asked if I had done any porn he could see me in.

I'm kidding!

He *didn't* ask me about porn.

Anyway, he was very nice, almost seeming too nice. If I didn't know any better, I would have thought he was hitting on me right in front of his wife, Elaine LaLanne. I think that is my all-time favorite name, Elaine LaLanne. I told one of the other workers what was transpiring, and he also thought Jack might have been hitting on me. Who knows? It must have been impossible to be "out" way back in the 1950s, especially if you had your own physical fitness show and the macho image that Jack LaLanne had.

He was over ninety when this happened, so if he were hitting on me, I would have declined. Though maybe, if he was two decades younger, Elaine LaLanne may have ended up a divorced woman and I would have ended up with a free lifetime membership to Jack's club, which later became Bally's, which later became L.A. Fitness, and to which I do belong.

Valerie Harper

Rhoda from *The Mary Tyler Moore Show* was a sweetheart. Shortly after she was diagnosed with cancer, she was at a cancer fundraiser. I was passing hors d'oeuvres and went up to her with a tray of mini Mediterranean salads, which was a tiny cucumber slice with chopped onion and tomato, topped with an olive. I asked, "Would you like a mini Mediterranean salad?" And she said, "Served by the Mediterranean man!"

She was observant to pick up I am an M.D. (Mediterranean Dude). I'm half Turkish, but she didn't know that. She was just being friendly and funny.

I was so sad when Valerie Harper passed away in August 2019 at the age of eighty. You could tell she was well loved by the posts people put on Facebook. Seemed everyone who met her liked her. I could tell in those few moments how warm a person she was.

Suzanne Somers

Sometimes we had to drive far for an event. Probably the only people who do more driving than caterers are truck drivers, racecar drivers, and Uber and Lyft drivers. You could say catering sucked the life right out of my car, too.

For one event, we drove all the way to Palm Springs which takes two hours and fifteen minutes with no traffic and five hours with traffic. I exaggerate, but you get my drift. Anyway, the event was at Suzanne Somers's house for her book-signing party. Suzanne loved us the minute we walked in. She thought we were the band and she was really nice to us; then she found out we were the caterers and was still nice to us, just not as excited. She ended up singing several songs with the band and was very good.

She lived next door to Barry Manilow who was not there. I guess she didn't follow the rule to always invite the neighbors when you have a party so that no one complains about noise. It would have been cool if Barry had been at Suzanne's, but I guess she could smile without him.

Monica Horan

She played Amy, Robert's wife on *Everybody Loves Raymond,* one of my all-time favorite TV shows. She was one of the most pleasant people I ever worked for. I just worked once in her house for a dinner. After the event, she was chatting with us like we were old friends. Just very sweet, very nice, and down to earth.

Doris Bleachman

Not sure I can say her real name, so I will call her Doris Bleachman. *Hint:* One of her lines in a Mel Brooks movie was "Yes, he vas my boyfriend" —said in a very thick German accent—and she was also on a show with the late Valerie

Harper. While I love her work, as she is truly talented and funny, meeting her in person was a letdown.

Doris had come up to the buffet and we didn't know who she was, just this pushy woman, and the buffet was not open yet, but a few were open in the back of the room. We had our station closed because it was near the stairs where the guests were entering, and we didn't want the 600 people coming up the stairs to get backed up all in the one place.

We were directing people toward the back to the other buffets. But Doris proceeded to just open up the lids by herself and take food. We told her repeatedly that we weren't open and that she should go to another, open buffet station. But she ignored us and continued to take food out (with her hands no less), not even using tongs.

I told the captain what she was doing and that she was ignoring my directions and Doris said, "I'm annoying you?"

"No, I said you were ignoring me when I said the buffet is closed."

The captain behind the buffet got on his walkie-talkie radio and said, "I need security right away." (He may have over-reacted, as we really didn't need security.)

We had no idea who she was, but honestly, it didn't matter because she was rude. I have LOW tolerance for HIGH-maintenance people.

One of the supervisors came out and looked at her and said, "Oh, it's Doris Bleachman, just let her eat." We had no idea it was her till he said that.

I actually love Doris' work. She's very funny and talented. I love the fact she did *Dancing with the Stars* at eighty-four years old. If she had said nicely, "I am an old woman and it's hard for me to walk all the way over there," maybe we could have accommodated her.

Although she looked like a woman in her sixties, if I had known her actual age I customarily would have been happy to let her take from the buffet. But she was rude.

When you disrespect me when I am doing my job, you get no respect from me.

OJ Before the Bronco Ride

About a year before the famous OJ Simpson Bronco chase, I served the table where OJ Simpson was seated for his friend's son's bar mitzvah. Looking back on it, it was one of his lawyer's sons who defended him at his trial. The event I worked was held at the Kaufman Astoria Studios in Queens, New York.

OJ was very nice and friendly and was letting everyone get pictures with him. A year later, he was on trial for the brutal murder of his ex-wife Nicole and her friend Ron Goldman.

Sarah Palin

I worked a fundraising event on a big naval vessel in California in 2010. Gene Simmons sang the national anthem, Sharon Stone spoke, an American Idol runner up also sang, and Sarah Palin spoke.

Palin spoke for at least twenty minutes and I have no idea what she said. Even the audience, which was mostly Republican, "her peeps" so to speak, didn't have a clue what she was talking about. It was like she was just throwing words out in incoherent sentences. I went up really close to her just to make sure it wasn't Tina Fey putting us all on.

Nope, it was Sarah.

This was after she and John McCain had lost. I'm trying not to make this book political, just calling it as I see it. But after seeing and hearing Sarah speak live, I'm even more at a loss of why some people thought she was a good candidate for VP.

A Tip from Ivana Trump

No, the tip wasn't "Don't ever marry an egotistical narcissist with orange hair."

Tips are sometimes one of the great perks of doing catering. Unfortunately, some catering companies keep the tip that is supposed to be divided among their waitstaff. We worked an event in Ivana Trump's apartment about twenty-five or so years ago. It was after she and Donald were divorced. I don't even remember who the caterer was, but he was known for not giving the tip to the staff.

Well, at the end of the event, Ivana comes out with a big wad of bills and hands it to the caterer in front of all of us and says, "This is for your staff." Because she did it in front of us, he knew he had to give us something. He went in the back "to add up and figure out." He came out a short while later and we all were tipped out a whopping $20 apiece. We knew we were supposed to get much more than that. For a job like that we would usually get a $50 to $100 tip.

Everything was made of gold in the apartment, even the toilet in the bathroom. We knew Ivana was more generous than that, even though this event took place after she left "The

Donald," who would become the forty-fifth president of the United States, a fact that may have sucked the life out of me even more than catering.

Tom Arnold

I was working an event in Hollywood, and, as I was passing around hors d' oeuvres, came up to Tom Arnold. This was an issue. Why? Because about six months prior to this he was in the movie I cowrote and produced with Tom Archdeacon, *Walk a Mile in My Pradas*. I was a little embarrassed, although there really was no reason to be, to go up to him now and serve him food. I said hello and reminded him who I was (we only had him on set for two days) and I joked, "Until the movie makes some money here I am doing this."

Tom was very nice and said, "I get it, you're doing what you have to do. Nothing wrong with that." And he was right. He was great to have in my film, he did a good job, and even improvised a little in it. I hope to run into him on more sets and not catering gigs. The film, which is on Amazon Prime, also stars the late Nathaniel Marston, Dee Wallace, Mike Starr, Bruce Vilanch, and Jason Stuart, who were all also wonderful to work with.

Patrick Dempsey

Patrick Dempsey was at a catering event I did a few years ago. I was coming out of the bathroom as he was entering, and I probably said something like "Next." I actually would have liked to have chatted with him, and would have, if he had not been going to answer Mother Nature's call. I had worked on a film with him twenty-plus years previously, before he did *Grey's Anatomy,* called *The Emperor's Club.* We worked on it a whole week.

Patrick was very nice. I actually had run into him a year after that on another set where I was just doing background work as a pedestrian. (I'm an excellent walker.) He remembered me and came up and said hello and we chatted for a few minutes. That was so cool for him to remember me. The name of his character in the movie *The Emperor's Club* was Masudi and my legal name is Sudi, so every time someone said the character's name I wanted to answer, and it was a little confusing on the set. I told him my legal name is Sudi even though I go by Rick.

We were just supposed to be background: classmates at a reunion. But they made us sing an original alma mater song, so we were upgraded. I still get residuals for that movie twenty-five-plus years later. It had been so long between that last set I worked on with him until that catering job that I knew he wouldn't recognize me. But if I'd had a chance to chat for a minute or two I believe it would have jogged his memory.

Obama Shook My Hand

When Barack Obama had just begun his campaign to run for president the first time I had barely heard of him. I found myself working in a house for a fundraiser for him attended by about forty guests. We served the courses, and then he got up to speak. I had never seen him before. I was so impressed with how he spoke and how sincere he sounded. I thought to myself, *He seems too nice and honest to be a politician.*

We finished serving and his people were rushing him out to catch a flight and he said, “Hold on.” Then he came around and shook all our hands and said, “Thank you.” There were no cameras, so he wasn’t doing it just for show. It was genuine and you could tell he was grateful. I think he got my vote that night.

Ron Raines

When I was in college at SUNY Plattsburgh, I did the play *The King and I.* The actor Ron Raines was a guest star. He played the king and I played Anna.

Kidding.

I played Luntha and Kristine Champine (now Klett) with whom I have remained friends, played my lover, Tuptim. Ron’s wife, Dona Vaughn, directed it. Sometime later, I took voice lessons from her.

Cut to several years later. Ron had become a very successful Broadway/TV star and I was working an Emmy’s party in Hollywood and there he was. It had been many years, but he was so glad to see me and I was glad to see him. He was up for an Emmy for his work on *Guiding Light*. So we were chatting away, but I was a little nervous because we are always told by the catering company, “Don’t speak too much to the stars” and “Be friendly to the guests but not too friendly,” but I knew him and we were having a really nice conversation. The entire time, I kept imagining that a captain was going to come up to me and demand I stop and that I would be reprimanded.

This reminds me of a similar story that another waiter experienced at an event attended by Hillary Clinton. He had previously played the King and Hillary had played Anna.

Again kidding.

He was working at an event, and she was there, and he had worked in the past on one of her fundraising campaigns, maybe when she was running for the Senate. At this event, Hillary kept looking at him like "I know you from somewhere" and she finally waved him over closer to her.

The captain saw my coworker walking toward her and freaked out and rushed over, but security stopped him. Meanwhile, they let the waiter right through and go up to Hillary.

She said "I never forget a face. Where do I know you from?," When he told her, she said, "That's right! Thank you again for your help."

Meanwhile, the captain fumed. When the waiter returned to his work, the captain tried to scold him. "How dare he just walk up to Hillary Clinton?" The waiter told the captain, "She waved me over and the secret service let me go over, and I'm a black man. You think they are just going to let a strange black man approach Hillary Clinton? She remembered me from when I helped on her campaign."

The irate captain was made speechless. I wish I had witnessed this when it happened.

Heart (Ann and Nancy Wilson)

I got off work and into a service elevator that Ann and Nancy Wilson and their manager happened to be riding in.

They had just finished performing at the event that I did not happen to catch. But I had just seen them on TV a few weeks previously singing an amazing version of "Stairway to Heaven" at the annual Kennedy Center Awards.

I told the Wilsons I loved their performance. They said nothing, gave half a smile, but the manager chimed in and said, "Thanks, we appreciate that."

They could have said, "Thank you," but they probably thought I was beneath them so "why even utter the words."

Listen up, celebs! You never know who's going to write a book, so be nicer to people. Silence can be as loud as thunder when it comes across as rude. You'd be nowhere without your fans, and since your band's name is Heart, you should really show you have one.

In their defense, maybe Tom Arnold told them I am a nut job.

John Cougar Mellonhead

I was not working the event when the following incident occurred. I heard it from others with whom I work, so it's hearsay and "their say," but this is pretty close to what happened.

Johnny C was smoking a cigarette inside, which is not allowed. The captain of the event went up to him and, with his thick French accent said, "Sir, I need you to put your cigarette out." He asked him a few times and was pretty much ignored.

The captain went up to him one last time with a glass of water and asked him to put it out in that, and "Mellonhead" said, "Ask me again and I'll put it out on your f#@* head."

What a douchebag!

I can't stand people who are that entitled. People who don't respect others who are doing their job, or those around them who have to inhale their second-hand smoke. They think they are better than everyone else.

I guess when you are born in a "Small Town" (I'm sure you are picking up on a pattern here) you have a small head and heart, too. Speaking of hearts, John C actually had already had two heart attacks from smoking when this went down.

The guy has done a lot of work for charities like Farm Aid. I appreciate him helping farmers and I like his music, but his behavior at this event was unacceptable.

Bowie's Birthday

I worked David Bowie's fiftieth birthday party in New York City. I was the server for his table. (The actor Matt Dylan was at the next table smoking a doob.)

David was nice. His wife, Iman, well, not so much. David didn't sit down at all to eat, just stood and chatted with friends most of the time. His plate was sitting there for quite some time, so his "lovely wife" obnoxiously says, "Take this plate away, it's cold."

Of course, it was cold! We had put it down fifteen minutes earlier and he hadn't sat down. A simple "Could you please bring a fresh plate? This one is cold," would have been as easy to say—but some folks have no manners.

She may have been a model, but she was not a good ROLE model.

Barbara Eden

I worked a lunch in the early '90s in Connecticut and Barbara Eden (yes, from *I Dream of Jeanie)* was at a table. One of the guys working with us was all excited and was telling us how much he loved her and begged us to let him serve her table, so we did. Everyone had finished their salads and he asked to take her plate and she said, "Not unless you want to lose an arm."

He started saying, "Oh, I'm so sorry" and she laughed and said, "I'm just kidding."

We were all dying laughing. It showed she had a great sense of humor.

Dolores Hope

Thanks to my friend Carl Hajik, I worked a few times in Bob Hope's house after he had passed. His widow, Dolores, lived there. A very sweet lady. At one of the events, at the youthful age of ninety-eight, she played a song on the piano and sang and sounded wonderful and full of energy.

I worked a couple of catering jobs there and they also hired me to work Dolores's hundredth birthday party—not to do catering, but to stand in a costume from the early 1900s next to a kiosk from that decade. I did not have to serve hors d'oeuvres but was told I was allowed to eat them. It was an easy, fun gig. The actress Gloria Stuart from the movie *Titanic,* who was close to that age as well, was there. I was standing behind them in front of the kiosk as the paparazzi was taking pictures of them.

I suppose you could call it a sort of photo bomb (before the term was popular) but really I was just standing where I had been placed.

Later I was also hired to work there for their daughter Maureen's birthday party, to participate in a fun *Wizard of Oz* sketch (as she was a huge fan). One of the last remaining munchkins from the film was in it with us and was about ninety-four at the time.

The Flying Nun, Had to Run (to the Restroom)

Sally Field asked me where the bathroom was after the Oscars. I actually did background work in the film *Legally Blonde 2* with her in a scene, but I'm sure she didn't remember me.

Babs

I worked an event in the backyard of a home where Barbra Streisand was a guest. She saw a little stage set up and asked me if there were going to be performers or speeches. I said, "I don't know, I just work here, today."

No, I didn't really say that. I said, "You and I are going to be singing 'You Don't Bring Me Flowers' together."

Okay didn't say that either.

I said, "Yes, I think so."

About twenty years before that, I did background work on a movie she directed, *The Mirror Has Two Faces*. I'm sure she didn't remember me from that.

Can't Have Your Cake and See Clint Eastwood, Too

I worked an event years ago where we were told that at some point Clint Eastwood was supposed to be there. One of the waiters was excited because he loved Clint and couldn't wait to see him. The event went on for a few hours with no sign of Clint. We served the first course, then the main course and he was nowhere to be seen. Finally, we served the desert, some kind of cake.

Right after the desert was put down in walked Clint Eastwood. He walked around the room saying hello to guests and shook a few hands. The waiter who was so excited to see Clint was nowhere in sight. Clint spent about ten minutes there and, boom, he was gone.

A minute after he left, I saw the waiter come out of the kitchen. I said, "Where have you been? You just missed Clint."

He said "What? Stop kidding around."

I said, "I'm serious, he just went around the room. Where did you go?"

He replied, "I was in the kitchen trying the cake."

I said, without missing a beat, "Well, you can't have your cake and see Clint Eastwood too."

He was so upset.

A Few More Celebs

I don't really get star struck, but it is cool to see stars up close sometimes, especially ones I've admired. Here are some other stars I came in contact with.

- ***Kevin Bacon*** came up to my buffet once when no one else was around. He was impressed at how I ordered more chicken with my headphones and walkie-talkie radio. It's amazing how important walkie-talkies or headsets make people look. I told him, "Believe me, what you do is much more interesting and here's one of my scripts." Kidding. We weren't allowed to give headshots or scripts to guests for obvious reasons. Does this count as a six-degrees of that Kevin Bacon thing?
- ***Elton John.*** I worked a charity luncheon about twenty-five years ago in NYC and had Elton John at my table. "The Rocket Man" was very nice and polite. This was after he stopped drinking. He finished every morsel on his plate and then we sang "Don't Go Breaking My Heart" together. I'm kidding of course. We actually sang, "Don't Let the Sun Go Down on Me."
- **Adam Sandler** came up to my buffet once. It was in a small VIP section and no one else was around. He was very nice, polite and friendly. He thanked me for helping out. Sometimes the bigger the star, the more attitude you expect, and you are pleasantly surprised when they are down to earth.
- **Phyllis Diller.** We were finishing setting up the room. Her son wheeled her into the room in a wheelchair before any other guests had come in. She was about ninety-five years old but full of energy and her laugh was infectious. Wish I would have spoken to her. I just

kind of looked on in awe. She passed a year or two after that.

- **Maroon 5.** Many times, I worked at the Pacific Design Center, or as another waiter called it, the Pacific Disaster Center. This one time, I had to bring some things to the green room for Maroon 5 who performed that night. They were kind of new. Their first CD was just out, and I had no idea who they were. They sang a few songs and were really good. The next day I found their music in the library. Since then I've bought several of their CDs.
- **Ryan Seacrest.** I worked in his house for a fundraiser. This was after the first several seasons of *American Idol*. He was nice and was talking more to us than the guests because the fundraiser was for someone's organization of which he knew few members. At many events, I go around singing to myself, but at this event I didn't. Wouldn't have wanted Ryan to think I was auditioning for the show.

  Speaking of *American Idol*, I once served an hors d'oeuvre or two to Adam Lambert at a different event a year or so after he was on *American Idol.* He was very polite. This was before he sang with Queen.
- **Amy Klobuchar.** In 2019, I worked a democratic fundraiser where the speakers were Amy Klobuchar and Pete Buttigieg. Amy came back into the kitchen to personally thank the waitstaff for helping out. She said one of her first jobs was as a waitress and she appreciated all we were doing. She seemed genuine

and that was nice of her to do that. Shows a human side of someone you might not see on TV.

- **Diana Ross** came up to the buffet in the VIP section. Many of the stars had an assistant or someone go up for them, but she came up herself. As she approached, I yelled, "Stop in the name of love."

  By now you know I'm not serious. It was self-serve and she asked, "Do we just serve ourselves?" I said, "Yes." She was very pleasant and not Diva-ish at all, which came as a bit of a surprise to me.

- **The "Stone."** I was assigned to the Stone and his entourage in the VIP section for an event. Served him and his friends drinks for hours. No tip! You shouldn't need a thesaurus to figure out his real name.

FIVE

CATERING 101

For those of you who picked up this book because you are thinking of getting into catering if after reading this chapter you still want to get into catering, I have not done my job in explaining it properly. Kidding.

Cocktail Hour (and the Grueling Hours That Follow It)

Since the cocktail hour is only one hour, you would think that doesn't seem too long, but believe me, it *feels* long, especially when it goes an hour and a half, sometimes even two hours. As I always say, "Two hours at work can drag by so slowly but *twenty years* goes by in the blink of an eye. *Whoosh!"*

The cocktail hour is fun for guests especially when they first enter. They are immediately greeted with a tray of wine or champagne or a specialty drink. It's not great for the schmuck holding the tray though. Those trays may look light, but after about half an hour of holding them, they feel like thirty pound weights. .. Sometimes the butler or waiter has to stand there for a good fifteen minutes—well really, a *bad* fifteen minutes, before any guests even enter. And while fifteen minutes can save you 15 percent or more on your car insurance according to Geico, fifteen minutes or more of holding a tray of glasses can give waiters' carpal tunnel syndrome.

The cocktail hour seems to last for days when passing the same thing over and over.

"I'll Pass"

When we pass hors d'oeuvres, we go up to the guest and say, "Would you care for some whatever it is?" Of course, we don't say *Whatever it is.* We tell them what it is (unless we forgot), then we say, "Would you like some?"

Sometimes the guest will say, "I'll wait," which is stupid because we may never make it back that way again. Sometimes they say, "No thanks." Sometimes they say, "Thanks," and take one. Sometimes they take two. And sometimes they just ignore you.

Sometimes they say, "I'll pass," meaning they don't want any, at which point I joke, "No, no, I'll pass. You stay here and have a good time." Many times, the guest will laugh at that line. If they don't laugh, the rest of the event I conveniently run out of hors d'oeuvres before I get to them.

Not really.

I put a scene in my movie, *Walk a Mile in My Pradas,* where the waiter, played by Felipe Pina, is passing quiche and when the guest says, "I'll pass," the waiter hands him the tray and says "You'll pass? Oh good, 'cause I have a lot of work to do in the kitchen." The waiter then walks away, leaving the guest holding the tray.

One of the food items we passed when I was a butler was mini cheeseburgers otherwise known as sliders, or as I call them, "Honey, I Shrunk the Cheeseburgers." Another item was pizza that was cut up in small slices, which we had to serve with two forks French service-style while holding napkins and the plate at the same time. This was quite the balancing act!

Other items included tuna tartar (and when I passed that I would say, "Get it while it's cold"), filet mignon on a crostini, duck in a bao bun (which I would apologize for serving during wabbit season and not duck season), and chicken skewers.

Attack of the Famished Guests

At some events, the guests come hungry, very hungry, as if they haven't eaten in weeks. They wait to pounce as soon as the server exits the kitchen with a tray of hors d'oeuvres. They plant themselves where the servers enter the room, salivating like Kujo, the killer dog, ready to attack. Then they may stop you quite a few times and empty your tray before you can get to the guests in the back of the room, who have not seen one morsel. To get to those guests in the back, there is a trick. Hold the tray high in the air with your arm extended, out of reach, and walk by briskly saying, "Special order" or "contaminated," or something like that.

One time in New York, my friend Tom Laughlin, who now owns his own catering company, was trying to get by this woman who had eaten enough food to feed an army to that point. He held the tray high in the air above his head as he rushed by her. Not taking the hint, she grabbed his arm, sending the tray flying with all the food landing on the floor. He turned and said to her, "Are you really that hungry?"

You would think the woman would have been embarrassed and laid low after that, but no, she continued zoning in on him and fed her face as he walked by.

The following story was shared by my friend Carl Hajik with whom I used to cater.

> *Whenever we worked the Pacific Design Center and tray-passed to the guests who seemed to be starving as always after a film viewing, I called it "Feeding pigeons in the park" because that's what it felt like. The guests would swarm around me like pigeons in the park during feeding time and I would straighten my arm out to them as they all would devour everything, then they all scattered away from me until the next tray of food was brought out.*

We worked many Screen Actors Guild screening receptions there. I've actually been both a guest and a server at these SAG events. Not at the same time, of course, although I am a Gemini, so I suppose I could've. I've been an actor and a SAG guest for the screenings and sometimes I worked for a caterer who did those events. They were filled with hungry actors coming out of a two-hour movie screening and half hour Q&A with the cast.

No popcorn was served during the movie, so when they got out they were hungry! They were upon you like a moth to a flame or like brown on rice (I know most people say "white on rice" but I like to be different), as soon as you brought out the tray. There was only one entrance into the room so "greedy guests" would be right there waiting to jump and attack as if they hadn't eaten in weeks. They were actors—so maybe they hadn't. The room would be overcrowded so it was hard to move past the first twenty people to serve others in the room.

I would usually see other actors I knew at these events. I preferred to see them when we were both guests, rather than asking them, "Would you like a teriyaki chicken skewer?"

"You People Are Crazy"

I once was a guest at an event where the waiter became so frustrated at people grabbing food that he finally came out and just put the tray on the floor. The guests picked the food off the tray on the ground. The waiter picked up the empty tray and screamed, "You people are crazy!" then went in the back. I'm not sure if he came out again.

I have to admit, sometimes it is the caterers' fault because they have an event with over one hundred guests and yet send the server out with a tray of only six chicken skewers. What do they expect?

When you are passing a tray of hors d'oeuvres, you're supposed to know exactly what you are serving and what it's called. Some items are hard to pronounce. Of course, those would be the ones that guests would make you repeat three times.

One of the items we used to serve that was hard to pronounce was foie gras. Fortunately, they stopped serving it because it was cruel to the animals. Foie gras is the liver of duck or goose fattened by cruelly force-feeding corn down a feeding tube into its gut.

The Setup

While some of the staff are serving the guests during the cocktail hour, the others finish setting up the room for when the guests come in. Pouring water in the glasses, putting bread and butter on the tables, and sometimes presetting the salads, and so forth. At events with a crowded cocktail hour, preset is the preferred assignment.

Types of Table Service

The following are some different types of service.

Sweep the Room

No, we didn't use a broom for this! *Sweeping the room* means starting at one end of the room and each server brings two plates at a time to the tables. There would be a "placer" on the floor with his or her arm in the air so you could see which table we were serving. It helped when the placer was tall so you could see through guests who were standing. The placer would point, and you would put the plates down where the placer pointed.

Pardon My French (While I Do French Service)

When I first started catering, it seemed like most events required French service. You had to go around to each guest, carrying a heavy tray, and serve them with two regular forks so that they could hold on to the piece of meat or whatever you were serving.

Why use regular tongs, which would make it easier to serve and be less likely to drop something?!

Then you might have to squeeze in between the two guests with this heavy huge tray, sweat dripping from your forehead, trying not to spill anything on the guest's lap. It could be brutal. Even for me who went to a gym and worked out regularly.

Most events I did were buffets or a plated dinner service where you just have to bring two plates at a time to a table and sweep the room in a group, which is pretty easy. Sometimes service is done family style, which means you leave all the dishes on the table (where nine times out of ten there isn't enough room to do this) and then the guests pass the platters around and serves themselves.

Restaurant-Style Switch-Out Service

This is the worst form of service at a catered event. The caterer I worked for was clueless that it never worked for various reasons. When two people finished their meal, the waiter took those two plates to the scullery (the bussing area that the dirty plates and glasses were brought back to) which is usually in the opposite direction of where you pick up the next course, way across on the other side of the room. Then you go in the kitchen, wait in a long line and pick up the next two plates, bring them to the table and set them down. Then you clear two more plates and go all the way to the other side of the room to put those in scullery, and then all the way back to the other side to pick up the next two.

You wait so long in the kitchen that half the guests finish the meal, while the other half are still waiting for their plate.

Buffets

My favorite form of service when catering is working behind a buffet. I love buffets. Always have. When I was born, the doctor spanked me, then they gave me a bottle of milk, which I quickly threw to the ground. I said, "This is not enough! Take me to a buffet!"

When I was a kid and my parents drove us down to Florida from Long Island, I remember we would stop at Sweden's Smorgasbord with buffets full of food, and I was hooked. In Florida, they had Shoney's which also had a buffet. In California, there's Hometown Buffet, which I used to go to a lot. I was going less and less, and then, in 2020, all buffets were closed due to the coronavirus pandemic.

Funny story. I was once at a Hometown Buffet in California for dinner and there was a wedding going on there. My friend kinda made fun of the wedding party, not to their faces, but to me. I thought, *Hey, this is what they can afford. Everyone will have enough to eat.* It was funny, though, seeing a woman in a wedding dress at a Hometown Buffet.

I only went on one cruise in my life, but if you've been on one of those, you'll appreciate that they always have a plethora of buffets.

As much food as they have at buffets and at catering events, every once in a while you still have a guest who is not happy with the amount of choices at the buffet. And sometimes we have three different types of buffets with all kinds of different foods at each buffet. Some people are just never satisfied, or they have so many dietary restrictions they should just stay home. Whenever someone asked me if something were gluten free, I would say, "Yes, it's free. No charge for the gluten." After the dirty look they gave me, I gave them the real answer.

I love eating at buffets. Working them, I don't love or hate. It's better than passing drinks or bussing plates or running food through a crowded room with a heavy pan in your hands. You also look important wearing a walkie-talkie headpiece. And you stand there, which for me is great, though for those who are hyperactive, it is a nightmare. Overall, it's not too bad except at events with music so loud that you and the expeditor, the person in the kitchen you are speaking to on the walkie-talkie who's relaying what you need to the chefs, can't hear each other.

There is an art to working the buffet. Like comedy, timing is everything. Usually you call for more food when you have 50 percent left in the pan, but there are many variables, like how far your buffet is from the kitchen, how many people are in line at the buffet, and how slow or fast the line is moving.

Actually, it's never fast. Many people pick this time to stand there and chat with each other while the line gets longer and longer behind them.

Some items also may take longer to prepare, like pasta, so you allow for more time for replacing that kind of dish. There is a real science to it. You almost had to do a mathematical equation to time it out so that when the food arrived, there were maybe four or five pieces left. They used to allow you to "marry the food," which meant put the new chafer pan in and then add the leftover food from the old one, but they stopped that, which really wastes a lot of food.

How to Get Fired from a Caterer

It's pretty hard to get fired. You have to screw up pretty bad, like get really drunk. Let me rephrase: You have to get *caught* getting really drunk. I was not one to drink at work. Actually, I am never one. I'm a Gemini, so I am always two. But I know a few workers who got fired for drinking, though several captains also drank, and some did stronger party materials, allegedly.

Getting into an argument with a captain could also get you gone. Or telling Billy Crystal, "The buffet is now closed." Apparently, a server got in an argument with him and he wrote a five-page letter to the caterer about it. That server was told the next day that her services were no longer needed.

Speaking of Cristal—okay, different spelling than *Crystal,* but I think I can still do a segue—a bartender put a bottle of Cristal champagne in his backpack to take home when the shift was over. I guess a captain needed an opener or something, so he went looking through the server's bag, found the champagne, and reported him. That guy ended up getting called into the office and yet *didn't* get fired because he claimed he didn't put it in there, someone else did, and told them they had no right to go through his bag.

Uniforms

When I first started catering, the uniform we wore was a full tuxedo. Then it changed to a blue Nehru jacket with black pants. This uniform was good because you could never tell if it was dirty and saved a lot on a cleaning bill. Then it was a "black bistro" outfit, which is black pants, a black dress shirt, a black apron, and a long black tie. Sometimes it was "white bistro," which is a white dress shirt, well-pressed. Crisp. (God forbid you have one wrinkle) Along with the rest of the black clothing above and shiny black shoes. It could be confusing at times, the going back and forth between a white bistro and a black bistro outfit, and unlike the Michael Jackson song, it DOES matter if it's black or white.

Inevitably someone would occasionally show up in the wrong color shirt, which is a worse feeling than you get when dreaming of showing up somewhere in your underwear.

Sometimes we also wore a white jacket, but not that often. It's kinda dumb to wear anything white when catering. White is like a magnet to red wine or meat sauce, so you're just begging to get something spilled on it. It's also stupid to wear a long black tie, and annoying, especially when it gets in the food, sauces, and the salad dressing bowl you are carrying to a table. Although a tie in the dressing makes for a well-dressed salad, I suppose.

And just to be cruel to the ones doing catering, they make you wear uncomfortable black shoes. And those shoes have to be well polished because if they are not, how will the guests be able to enjoy their food? The best is when they are shiny when you arrive for an event, but if it's outdoors, they end up with dust or mud on them, by the middle of the event.

With all the walking that butlers and waiters have to do, they should be permitted to wear sneakers.

Part of the uniform is also a wine key, a pen, and a lighter. If you were feeling rebellious, you would bring matches instead of a lighter.

When the outfit was a blue Nehru jacket, we had to wear tuxedo pants with the black stripe down the seam of it, not just plain black pants. One time, a butler didn't have tuxedo pants, just plain black pants, and he didn't want to get written up for not having the right pants, so he put black masking tape along the sides of his pants. One would have to look very, very closely to notice that it wasn't real and that it was tape.

There's always one or two captains who would notice something like this, and unfortunately for that butler, one of them was the captain that day and she noticed.

If you were working an outdoor summer event, the uniform might be "picnic attire," which was khaki pants and a white polo shirt with tennis shoes. "Set up attire," if you were setting up the event the day before, was jeans and a polo shirt.

SIX

PET PEEVES ABOUT GUESTS AND CLIENTS AND THE RULES OF CATERING

If you get nothing else out of this book, I hope this chapter will help make everyone a better guest at catered events and learn how to be on their best behavior so as to not drive the servers over the edge.

How Guests Annoy Servers

The following is a partial list (a full one could probably fill a whole book) of things guests do that annoy the servers to no end, or just make it more difficult to do a good job.

- A buffet is open for three hours and no one has come up to it in the last half hour, and then, just as we start breaking it a down, a group of people decide to rush the buffet.

- Same situation as above except for the bar. It's open for hours and then we close, but there are always those few who don't know what *closed* means.

  One woman came up to me at the end of an event. When I told her the bar was closed, she kept insisting a drink be served to her. I kept saying, "Sorry, no."

  She said, "Why not?"

  I said, "The bar is now closed."

  She said, "You can't just give me one drink?"

  I said, "That wouldn't be fair to everyone else."

  She pressed on, "Why are you being so mean?" Then she grabbed an already poured glass of wine from earlier on the bar.

  Before she could walk away, I grabbed it back.
- Guests who put napkins or garbage on the tray with which you are passing the hors d'oeuvres. Or worse, they put their used toothpick on the tray, leaving their germs for the next guest.
- When guests ignore the person serving them. The server comes up with a tray and asks, "Would you like one?" They look right at you and don't say a thing, don't nod, nothing. Or don't look at you at all. You're not there, you little peasant!
- When the butler is clearing the table and the guest has absolutely nothing on their plate but acts like, "How dare you ask if you can take my plate. I'm not finished." There is NOTHING on their plates. This applies to glasses without even a sip in them.

- Double dipping (Thanks to Seinfeld, everyone knows this one.)
- They ask you to bring a certain hors d'oeuvre to them from the kitchen when there are 500 guests. But yes, I'll make sure the chef gets right on that, and I will make sure I find you. *Not.*
- When guests move from the spot they were in after they asked you to bring something to them. So now you can't find them to give them the pain in the ass thing they asked for.
- Unlike Burger King, special orders *do* upset us!
- Leaning or pulling chairs out at tables to save them for later—in other words, leaving the legs sticking out so someone can trip on them.
- Asking two or three different servers for the same thing instead of waiting for the first one to bring what you asked for. As a result, the waiter brings the drink you asked for and finds two other fresh drinks sitting there.
- Standing right near the kitchen and stopping the waiter every time he comes out with a new hors d'oeuvre to get something, even though most of the other guests at the party have not gotten any yet because these gluttonous guests block the waiter every time and hogging all the food.
- Don't ask more than once what the server is passing. Listen the first time. Or if the same item has come out a few times, you should know what it is already. My friend Kim Kadel told me once she had been out several times with the same thing and the guest kept making

her repeat it. After an hour of serving the same thing enough times that they should have known what it was, when they asked for the fourth time, Kim said, "It's shit on a shingle, you want one?"

- If you have more than three allergies or you are a complete vegan, bring your own food or stay home.
- When you are going through the buffet line, keep in mind there are five or ten or twenty people behind you in line. Don't stop and chat for ten minutes. You're slowing down the line. Just take a plate of food and go. Some people spend an eternity trying to decide what they want. It's not the life and death situation that some make it out to be. Just take the f@*&^g chicken and eat it!
- Make sure your eyes are not too big for your stomach. Take what you can eat. Don't waste food. (That's the caterer's job.)
- Guests who are really early and expect special service.
- Guests who are really late and expect special service.
- Guests who are on time and expect special service.
- A guest asking to pack food up for them in someone else's house. It's supposed to go to the host. (Contributed by Susan Bennett.)
- Guests ignoring you as you are trying to set down their meal and you need them to move their arm or something. Sylvester Stallone did this once, and finally the person next to him got his attention to move his steroid-filled arm.

- Guests that don't leave. The "hanger ons" that you just want to hang. Take the hint! Everyone else is gone, the bar has been broken down. Like the Jordan Peele movie says, GET OUT! At one of the places where we worked many events, there was a guy in charge, Mitch Hara (currently starring in *Smothered* on Amazon Prime with Jason Stuart), who was really strict about this. If the party ended at 10 PM, then at precisely 10 PM he would pull tablecloths right off the table in front of the guests. He would grab their drinks even if they weren't done. The party was over. "BOOM, everybody out!"
- Guests who want tea instead of coffee. I like tea also and I don't even drink coffee, but it is much more of a pain to get tea than coffee at events. Also, the really annoying folks who want a very specific flavor like non decaf, herbal, blah, blah, blah.
- Guests who ask for cappuccino or latte or expresso. Just NO. We don't have that. We are not a Starbucks. Just drink your decaf.
- Guests who ask if we are sure it's decaf. No, we are not, but it is annoying when you ask. Actually, we usually are sure. Half the time it's "magic pot," which means only decaf was made, but we say it's both. Sue us.
- Guests who drink coffee.
- Guests who ask to get their picture taken or the whole table's picture taken. "Sure, no problem. I only have forty plates to bus and have to pour wine and water,

and bring out the next course, but sure let me stop and take your picture."

- When someone asks for one thing. The server brings it. Then they ask for another. Then the server comes back, and they ask for something else, so we have to make several trips.
- Asking for to-go boxes or containers, as most times there are no to-go containers.
- Special requests at the last minute for something that is not on the menu, or not easy to get or make. (This one is from Chef Keith Johnson.)
- Outrageous requests. Someone once asked Krysta Florczyk to walk their meal across the street to where they lived during an ongoing event. She had to push a cart across the busy street in downtown L.A. following the guest to their home. The guest said they would bring back the cart, and Krysta said, "No, you won't. I'm taking it back now."
- Eating over the buffet. (This answer was contributed by Chef Marcos Rodriguez.)
- This one has been said already, but I love the way Tia Roberts puts it; she even uses a catering pun, which makes her okay in my book, literally: *"This one lumps my gravy and grinds my gears: When people attack you like sharks and don't allow other guests to have any food. The ones that wait outside the door ready to pounce on you. Ones that make you walk through the crowd with your plate high in the air, and STILL they want more. They have zero social graces and act as*

though they haven't eaten in days. I want to f@%king CUT them!" P.S. Tia is now serving twenty years in prison for attacking a guest. (I'm kidding.)

Annoying Things the Client Does

While guests do annoying things, sometimes the client actually is the worse culprit.

Last-Minute Changes

The biggest issue. Last-minute changes are SO frustrating. The whole room has been set up with the proper number of chairs at each table according to the seating plan. Then, as guests are being seated, they decide to add guests to the table or take them away. So now, in a crowded room, you have to remove or add chairs, silverware, glasses, napkins, and so forth when you are supposed to be greeting the guests at your table and offering them wine.

Sometimes just before an event starts, the client decides they want the bar or buffets to go somewhere else. We've spent two hours setting it up and it's next to impossible to move them with everything on it. So now, you have to remove everything, move the table, and reset everything on it. At one event, the host didn't like the bar that was rented which she had approved only days before. A few hours before the event was to start, she wanted another whole bar ordered after the first bar had already been set up.

The new one came only ten minutes before guest arrival did and everyone had to scramble to help the bartender take down everything from the first bar and replace it on the other. Total nightmare. Totally unnecessary.

Guest Count Way Over

When the number of guests is WAY over what the client said it would be. When this happens, you don't have enough servers to give the excellent service we are supposed to give and sometimes you run out of food. Or you have to wash dishes or glasses or silverware, as only enough was ordered from the rental company for the number of guests expected.

Making the Staff Wear Costumes

At some events, the client wants the staff in ridiculous costumes. My good friend JoAnna Frohn, who used to book staff for events, said she once had to dress up her staff in turbans. Another time, the staff had to wear contact lenses that looked either like cat's eyes or flames. Another time, she had to wear a blue hazmat suit. (I had to Google this since I didn't know what it was. After I did, I felt JoAnna's pain.)

She once staffed an event for Victoria's Secret, and they wanted all guys with 14½-inch necks. They wanted to do a "go see," which is kind of like an audition an actor or model normally does for print jobs. Ironically, given the company sells products made for women, they didn't want women serving at the event, so she had the women from her staff working in the back, pouring drinks, and so on.

The Catering Gym

Caterers are not moving companies, but you wouldn't know that from some of the events we've worked. Sometimes the client has the catering staff move furniture before and after a party to make room for the guests. You don't need to pay for a gym when you do catering, and many times you get more exercise at an event than during a workout at the gym.

Once in a while, you get an easy, cushy, job like being "the clicker." You just have to click in how many guests have come in and maybe greet them as they enter with a hello.

Another cake job I have done was "door watcher" during events at L.A. Live. The servers have to go up and down the back stairways to deliver food, and due to fire safety issues, someone has to sit in a chair making sure the door stays open on each floor the staff is using. The "watcher" can bring reading material, and it is one of the few times you can be on your cell phone. These easy types of assignments are extremely rare. And while the one lucky son of a gun sits in the chair, the other workers are going up and down several stairs or running heavy pans with food to the buffets.

Parking

Finding a parking spot is one of the biggest pains in the ass in Los Angeles and Hollywood. Every year I worked, it became worse and worse, and there would be less street parking. Many times, the caterer didn't pay for parking, so we'd have to park several blocks away, especially when we worked down in the L.A. Live area. You'd spend forty minutes driving to the area and then another half hour driving around blocks to find parking. I refused to pay for parking.

Several streets in Hollywood where you used to be able to park all day suddenly became only one-hour or two-hour parking. I probably lost about ten pounds a year walking to events. (I guess this could be a pro.)

Counting the Rentals

There was a caterer who required that all dirty rental linen, including hundreds of napkins, be counted at the end of the event. AND we had to count all the dirty utensils too. Gross! Meanwhile, it wasn't counted when it arrived, so if a few were missing at the end of the event, they might have never been there in the first place. This was a huge waste of time and money for the client who was paying to have all these workers do this stupid task. Sometimes, the caterer or client doesn't rent enough supplies, so you have to borrow some from the house, or from the caterer's own utensils. You have to know which is which, so that at the end of the night nothing goes to the wrong place.

Rules in Catering

The dos and don'ts of catering are:

- No cell phones on the floor.
- No eating on the floor.
- No talking on the floor.
- No moving or dancing to music on the floor.
- No having fun on the floor.

- No picture-taking of celebrities or in clients' houses. (This really shouldn't have to be said but there are a few idiots who do it.)
- No asking for autographs. (Like we really want their autographs?)
- No soliciting for acting work. Many times, when catering in L.A., guests are directors, and producers, but they are not at the event to talk to you about your acting aspirations.
- Be friendly but not too friendly. Be hospitable with the guests, smile, exchange a pleasantry or two, but the guests are not there to hear your life story.
- Serve from the left, clear from the right, pour from the right. (Put your right foot in and shake it all about.)
- Never say no to the client, even when the answer is no. *No* is a foreign language to many guests, which is ironic because the word *no* is the same in most languages, *yes?*
- Smile (unless you look like a serial killer when you do). Even in Hollywood, it's hard to be that phony and smile through some of the s#*t shows we've had to endure, but we try. They always tell us to smile, which I do naturally, because half the time I have gas. The captain at one event stressed over and over again how important it was for us to smile. Well, there was one worker who had a lazy eye or was cross-eyed and when he smiled he looked like a serial killer. He was serving behind a buffet and smiling his heart out. After a short while, the captain told him to stop smiling.

SEVEN

THE NIGHTMARES NOT ON ELM STREET

Most of the people who I've worked for in their houses were a delight. I've worked for many nice people, some of whom I became and remained friends with. Then there were the few who were horrible. I have changed the names in these stories to protect the not-so-innocent. Let's start with the worst.

I worked for a guy in California who would staff us at different events and houses. Most of his clients were lovely, very nice people and it was fine working in their houses. But there was one of his clients who will go down in the history books. Well, maybe not the history books, but she's going down in my book. What a bi-otch she was. And her name was . . .

Mrs. Oleson

No, not Nelly Oleson's mother from *Little House on the Prairie* (Nelly's mother was much nicer). I've changed this woman's name in case she reads this book. (I only left one letter off her name but according to Saul (I better call him soon), my attorney, that is enough to not get sued.

Mrs. Oleson lived in Beverly Hills. What a miserable woman, not happy with anything. Working for her was like walking on eggshells, as bad as being in an abusive relationship. I don't know how her kitchen staff put up with her. I'm surprised they didn't use the kitchen knives on her instead of cutting up her food. I had more patience than most who worked there, and I worked there at least six or seven times. You'd think she might warm up a little or be happy that she had someone good who knew what was expected, etc. NOPE.

You had to wear a tuxedo and white gloves and serve a five- or six-course meal while avoiding stepping on her precious dog who was laying on the floor near the table. No matter how good the service was, she was never satisfied. Her husband was fine and so were the guests. I thought she came from money, hence the attitude. Came to find out that she was working at a car dealership as a sales assistant or something and married a rich guy.

Here's one example of her obnoxious behavior. After Mrs. Oleson and her guests were served a five-course meal, they retired to the other room to have champagne, tea, and dessert. Everyone had some and I approached her with the bottle of champagne to offer a refill without her even asking me. I was being very attentive and proactive. I poured some in her glass and she said, "Is that all you're going to give me?" Not "Thank you," not "A little more, please." She was so ungrateful.

The straw that finally broke the "Turkish camel's back" and convinced me to stop working for her was a lunch I was asked to work where she was supposed to have four guests. It turned out to be nine guests seated outside in the heat, for whom I was serving five courses and constantly refilling the wine and water. Just me serving, wearing the stupid white gloves.

I had told the person who hired me to work there (for whom I was filling in at the last minute) that I would have to be done by 5:00 PM. I had to be somewhere at 6:30 PM. I think I was going to a Dolly Parton concert that night. I was told it was a lunch so that would be fine and that I should be done way before that time.

I started at 11 AM, served the five or six courses until it was now late afternoon, almost 5:30 PM. Everything was cleared except the water glasses. Most guests had gotten up and were sitting by the pool. At this point, it was half an hour after my promised out time. I went up to her and said, "I really have to go, I had told so-and-so who hired me that I had to leave at 5:00 PM and now it's almost 5:30 PM." She gave me this dirty look, and said in her annoying unappreciative voice, "I wish I knew there was some kind of time restraint." Mind you, it was a lunch gig and it was now 5:30PM. I gave excellent service for six hours. Everything was done except the few remaining water glasses left on the table.

I was livid. I think a vein popped out of my head. The husband noticed I looked a little miffed and came over and asked, "Is everything okay?" I explained to him that I had to go, everything was done. He said, "That's fine," paid me and tipped me. He was no problem at all.

I ended up writing a two-page letter to the guy who hired me to work for Mrs. Oleson explaining why I wouldn't work for her ever again. No one wanted to work there. I heard another waiter actually sent her a letter directly telling her off and explaining how awful she was. I would love to see that letter.

I know forgiveness is good, but I have decided to bash her in this book instead. Makes for a more fun read and is much more therapeutic and satisfying.

My Scathing Emails

I tend to write emails telling people off if they deserve it and Mrs. Oleson was someone who was deserving of one of my scathing emails. I sent the following email to the guy who hired me to work for Mrs. Oleson:

Subject: Why I will No longer work for Mrs. Oleson

I always walk away from the Olesons' house feeling degraded, frustrated, and resentful. Though the pay is very good, it's like walking on eggshells from the moment you get there till the moment you leave, and even when the party goes off without a hitch, Mrs. Oleson is ***never*** *satisfied.*

I should feel more comfortable the more I work in someone's home. There, it is the opposite. I do not feel comfortable working for her. She is extremely disrespectful and rude throughout the whole party, and it makes it more difficult to give good service.

***Mr.** Oleson was fine, the guests were fine, and Magdalena who works in the kitchen was great. (I am confident she would say I always do a good job and she might even say I have a good sense of humor.)*

Last Thanksgiving, I walked out of there with over $500, and it still wasn't worth what we were put through. I also worked a lunch, a five-course meal, nonstop, providing excellent service all by myself. Everyone was happy. I had to be somewhere at 6:30 PM, which I told you. There was nothing left to do, the guests were happy, but she was upset that I was leaving ***over an hour*** *past when I really needed to leave. Mr. Oleson, gentleman that he is, came over and said everything was fine, thanked me, and tipped me.*

I have been catering for over fifteen years and this is one of two houses I draw the line, and I really did give it a second, third, and fourth chance. I just cannot put myself through working there again.

Rick

Ms. Claudette Coin

I once had the DIS-pleasure of working at Ms. Claudette Coin's house in the Hamptons. This wasn't her real name and I could almost include her in the celebrity chapter, but I don't think most people would know who she was. They are better off. She was the gossip columnist on a live morning talk show way back in the 1980s. Now, I will gossip about HER.

She was the ex-wife of a famous billionaire. She was a pain in the ass, pardon my Turkish, I mean French, the few times I worked at her house. It was like walking on rotten eggshells. Very stressful. I don't know how people work there full time. I have too much self-respect to work full time for someone who doesn't respect me or looks down on me.

I worked at her house for a July Fourth weekend event. I was there the whole weekend. On July Fourth for the actual event there was one waiter for every two guests, so there were one hundred guests and fifty waiters. She wanted very detailed service. Better to be overstaffed than understaffed, I always say, but this was a little ridiculous.

Someone famous was there for breakfast one morning that weekend, and Claudette had stressed over and over and over to me to NEVER take a glass or plate without a tray. Never. I was walking by the table when her guest Regis Philbin asked me to take his plate away. I said, "Certainly, I'll be right back for that," and Claudette asked, "Why aren't you taking the plate?" I replied, "Because you specifically said don't take anything without a tray, so I'm going to get a tray." She said, "Oh just take the plate." You couldn't win with her.

At one point, I was in the kitchen getting coffee for a guest and her two butlers were nowhere to be found. Her phone was ringing (landline, this was before cell phones) and she was in there talking to her friend. The phone kept ringing and she said to me in a very snotty voice, "Would you get that?"

Now, mind you, I didn't normally work there, and answering phones wasn't in my contract. Okay, there was no contract, which means there was no NDA, hence this section in the book. Anyway, I picked up the phone and the woman on the other end of the line asked for Ms. Coin. I asked, "Who's calling?" The woman on the other end spoke so fast I couldn't understand her. So, I asked again who was calling. It sounded like she said, "Ms. Coin calling for Ms. Coin," which didn't make any sense. *She's calling for herself?*

Claudette asked me who it was, and I said, "I'm not sure." She said, "Well, you have to ask." Now, she had heard me ask twice already, so I asked a third time, and the woman said, "It's her mother." So, I said to Claudette, "It's your mother," and Claudette says, "Oh, I'll have to call her back."

The whole weekend went like that. Not a good experience.

Ms. Coin passed away several years ago, the younger one. I'm guessing the mom has also. So now she HAS to talk to her.

Coffee and an Alka-Seltzer

After working at Ms. Coin's house all weekend, I felt a little frazzled and uncomfortable by Sunday. Everything had to be perfect and I was so fed up with all the things we had to put up with. I was pretty much over it when the intercom in the kitchen sounded. "Hello? Hello? Anyone there?" For some reason, I was the only one in the kitchen again. I'm not sure where her two full-time butlers were but I finally picked up the intercom and said, "Yes, what the f*&# do you want now bi-otch?"

Ok, I didn't really say that. I said, "Yes?"

She said, "Where are my butlers?"

I said, "I don't know, it wasn't my turn to watch them." Kidding.

She whined, "I'm really tired and want something to wake me up, but my stomach is kinda bothering me, I don't know what I should have."

I said, "Well I can bring you a coffee with some Alka-Seltzer in it." She laughed.

When the butler came back, he was aghast that I'd joked like that with her, but then said she needs to laugh more like that. Watching this woman made me realize how unappreciative some people are with all that they have. That it's never enough. She was married to a billionaire and lived in a multimillion-dollar house. She still didn't seem happy.

This next story is also about her. Though I wasn't there to witness it, a friend who worked for her told me about it. This one really shows her lack of gratitude.

"Now I Have Nothing to Eat"

He told me about what happened at breakfast one morning. To set the scene, every morning Claudette Coin's staff put out fresh fruit, bagels, several cereals, and many different flavors of yogurt on a buffet. She also had her own private chef who could make her waffles, omelets, pancakes, hash browns, bacon, whatever her little cardiovascular pump (to call it a heart would seem factually wrong) desired. So, she called over the butler and asked him where the special-flavored yogurt was that she wanted. He told her that he went to three different stores and they didn't have it. She said, "Next time go to fifteen stores if you have to. Now I have nothing to eat."

If I had been there when she said this, I would have told her off. I would have said, "Really? You have all this food here and some people don't even have milk for cereal, and you say you have nothing to eat? How dare you, you spoiled ungrateful brat."

I know, I know, so easy to say things when you're not there.

EIGHT

HOW DO YOU (DIS) LIKE THEM ROTTEN APPLES?

I've actually worked for many caterers who are very friendly and treat the staff well. Then there are those who suck the life right out of you. They are toxic.

I had been California for about a year, and while on the set of a soap opera doing some background work, I spoke with a guy there named Derek Capozzoli. When I mentioned I did catering he said he could probably get me in with the caterer he worked for. They paid more than the one I had been working with. He referred me and I did get hired, and to this day, I don't know whether to thank him or kick him in the nuts.

Some companies I've worked for have one person that stands out as a horrible human being. Some might have two, but this one horrible company, in particular, had many—probably enough bad apples to fill up a whole orchard. Three women and one man there stood out as people who needed a lesson on treating people better.

The Bitches of Beastwick

These women and this one guy in the office somehow didn't know they were in the hospitality industry. Sure, they were nice enough to the clients (for the most part), but they treated the staff like something that is deposited in a toilet. I was taught that if you have nothing nice to say about someone, don't say anything at all. I was also taught algebra and calculus and don't remember those either. These three women were awful. The B word comes to mind and the C word (and these don't stand for *baking* and *cooking).*

Sharon (B)

I had worked for the company for over ten years and I could literally pass Sharon and say hello and she wouldn't even muster up a hello back. Once or twice she gave me a slight smile, but I am assuming she had gas. She was like this with all the staff. She would never say hello or have a conversation with you, but had no problem yelling at you once in a while. For example, one time we were outside in the pouring rain when the event came to an abrupt halt because of the inclement weather. As we were stacking chairs and putting away tables on the pool deck, she yelled at us to do it faster. I just looked at her and said, "Oh. My. God," and walked away. Had I not left, who knows what I would have said, but it would have been ugly.

I heard the following story about her. One time there was a young guy working with a party planner for three days in a row in conjunction with our company. On the third day, he went up to Sharon, as she was one of the salespeople. He was just being friendly. He put out his hand and said, "Hi, I'm so-and-so. Just wanted to say hello. I've been working here the last few days."

She said, "I don't need to know who you are, and I don't need to shake your hand."

The poor kid was upset by this. That one interaction tells you everything you need to know about this woman. She thought she was hot shit on a silver platter, but she was just a cold turd on a paper plate.

I came up with that expression. Quote me if you like.

Betty (B)

I really shouldn't make fun of someone's weight, and usually I don't, but when they are evil, it is easy to do. I know it's wrong. I am not perfect. I refer to Betty as this company's cash cow because, well, she does get them a lot of cash by getting clients, and well . . . never mind.

One day, Betty B, the large woman with a small heart who also always screams at everyone and can be very rude, fell in the middle of the kitchen floor, landing, BOOM, right on her big keister. *Keister* means buttocks, hiney, bottom, tush, gluteus maximus, for those who don't know. We were standing in line waiting for hors d'oeuvres.

Usually when someone falls like that, someone would ask, "Are you okay?" or they would go to help her up. But this woman was so mean to everyone that they all had to stifle a laugh. When she fell, one of the butlers, Claudio Luna, without missing a beat, said, "Is the floor alright?" It was hard to stifle our mirth after that.

Another time, this same woman got pizza thrown at her by someone who worked with a party planner. He had finally had enough, after dealing with her for twenty years. I was not there to witness this, but she said something that set him off and he said something along the lines of, "Listen you fat b&#*, I've put up with your s$#&* for twenty years," then threw a slice of pizza at her.

Amerilla

WCB caterers went through managers faster than Jennifer Lopez went through husbands. Then the company settled on one for several years who was absolutely horrible, Amerilla. She was one of the worst managers they ever had and was just a miserable human being. A tiny, short, little thing who made BIG problems for the staff. She had the personality of a toothpick. Not one of the colorful ones, but the plain wooden ones.

Amerilla did everything she could to make the workers lives more miserable, and everything she could to make the company more money by taking more away from the employees. She encouraged captains to write up the butlers for the stupidest things, then they were called into the office like they were in high school and had detention.

The first time I saw her (she never introduced herself as the new general manager to anyone) was at a meeting before an event. She went on and on about how bad a job everyone had been doing at recent events, and everyone had to step up their game. She had nothing positive to say. The captain, Dennis Richardson, threw in a positive comment after she was done so morale wasn't completely destroyed. Then the event began, which was way understaffed. I went up to Amerilla in the middle of the event and said, "This event is way understaffed."

She replied in her snotty way, "That's the way the client wanted it."

Well, how the hell are we supposed to do a good job if we are understaffed?!

God, she was so stupid and unfriendly! I would go on, but I don't like to talk bad about anyone. Who am I kidding? I love to talk smack about evil people. So, I will continue.

Amerilla said no staff could take food home at all. (It would be thrown out right in front of us.) Yet, she herself would leave with bags and boxes of food to take home to her little brats at home. Amerilla gave instructions not to let anyone who worked for the company know that we were allowed to get a certain amount of sick pay even though we worked for them only part time. We didn't find out for the longest time and if she had her way, we never would have.

She was evil.

One day karma met Amerilla. I heard her husband cheated on her and she left with her two kids to go back to her family in another state. Don't know if it's true, but this story makes me happy. She treated the staff so poorly. She got her "just desserts." (Those who keep track of all the catering puns in the book win a prize.)

Morey Seamstress

There was a guy at the same company who was a horrible man to work for. I'm not just throwing him in to prove I'm not a male chauvinist and have something against women bosses. He also treated the staff like crap. I later found out he was high on cocaine half the time.

Once, one of the captains wanted me to expedite in the kitchen with him and I said, "No thanks, I'll stay on the floor." No one else wanted to do it, so I guess she thought I have a good temperament, which I do, and could deal with him. He always talked down to the staff.

The worst thing is he stole our tips from events. One waiter even heard him bragging about it and how he bought the new jacket he was wearing with waiters' tips.

One event stands out the most with this prick. We were doing a setup for an event. The day before, we placed the tables, put all the linens on them, and unwrapped and placed the plates, silverware, and glasses. We set up the side stations, which would have the wine, coffee cups, water pitchers, extra silverware, and glasses on them. It's a lot of work and there were only a few of us doing it. It was outside and it got dark and cold toward the end, but we finished a seven-hour job in five hours. I signed out at the five hours, because if you go one minute over without a half hour break, there is a meal penalty to the company.

After I signed out, Morey said, "I just need you guys to fold some napkins," something the staff could do the next day before the event.

I said, "If we do, there's a meal penalty because we didn't have our break."

He said, "You guys sat down and ate for like forty minutes," with such an arrogant attitude.

My blood started boiling and I raised my voice just a little as I said, "We took a ten-minute break to eat and we just worked our asses off in the cold, setting up this whole event in record time." One of the other workers had asked me for a ride in my car, so I said to them I'll be in the car waiting, and I stormed off.

The next day, I got a call from the company that Morey had written me up for yelling at him in front of guests. There were no guests and I was off the clock, and I didn't yell. I raised my voice. So, I had to go into the office. They said it wasn't a big deal, that I'd never been in trouble before and that I should just sign the paper. I only signed it after I corrected on the form that there were no guests at the event, and that I was off the clock when the incident occurred.

I never should have signed it. The wench Amerilla tried to use it against me a year later. One of the other butlers wrote a letter on my behalf, defending me and pointing out what a douchebag Morey was. He didn't use the word *douchebag,* but the name fits, and I want Morey to wear it.

This is the letter my coworker wrote on my behalf:

My account of the event I worked with Rick. We were the only ones there, if the owner of the house was there, then he was inside the house, but I never saw him. We were working on the lawn, setting up which was scheduled to take seven hours, but we were pushed to finish in five.

Morey walked around and talked the whole time and was very rude, and in my opinion, out of character for someone in charge. I believe that if you are going to be in charge, you should be the first one to help and set a good example, not demean the employees and tell them that they are doing an awful job.

Somewhere in the setup process we were able to grab a quick bite to eat, but in no way did we get a full thirty minutes. Most of us had signed out but Morey was trying to make us stay off the clock to help and Rick stood up for us. Morey responded in a very demeaning way.

It is very unfortunate that we, as a crew, worked our butts off getting that event set up and the thing I remember is never being told that we did a good job, but getting abused verbally for not staying after signing out.

Event from Hell

The four people I just described, worked for a company that treated their staff like a bowel movement, and these four people exemplified all the toxic things that company stood for. The following is an email I sent to the company regarding one of the understaffed events: Like the Mueller report it has many redactions for anonymity in it, so they can't sue me.

How Catering Sucked the Life Right Out of Me

Hello,

This is regarding the event (Name of caterer REDACTED) they did from Thursday, Aug 9, till Sunday, August 12, 2012, for the (REDACTED). I only worked the event Friday and Sunday. (I was too sick from working in the heat on Friday to work Sat.) It can only be described as physical abuse and inhumane treatment and working under dangerous and nearly impossible conditions. Or as one butler put it "cruel and unusual punishment." It's amazing no one got heat stroke.

The main problem was it was ***severely*** *under-staffed all four days. Apparently the amount of staff was cut in half from the previous year with an increased guest count this year. When brought up to the general manager Amerilla that it was way understaffed, her reply was "Yes, we know that's the way the client wanted it."*

All china was used for the event for thousands of guests, so it was nonstop bussing of heavy bus tubs with limited workers, for over five hours in over 90-degree heat, wearing a long ***black*** *shirt, tie, and apron. This went on for four days. One of the butlers injured his shoulder from this but didn't say anything. In fact, all the butlers were complaining, but most were probably afraid to say anything for fear of losing their job, or getting written up, but someone has to say something, so that this unacceptable treatment to staff will not happen again.*

The event was overcrowded in the tent (which is a fire hazard) to the point where it was nearly impossible to get through the thousands of people. These were seven- to eight-hour shifts, and when we got our half-hour break there was no food for staff. By law, they ***don't have*** *to give you food, but there's really nowhere to go to get something to eat in that area of downtown L.A.. It would take fifteen minutes to walk to the one or two places to get an expensive meal and fifteen minutes to walk back, which uses up your break time.*

The ***right thing to do*** *would be to have sandwiches for the staff, or at least let them get something from the tasting going on at the event.*

Abraham Lincoln must have been turning over in his grave if he saw the almost slave-like labor going on at this event.

Sincerely,
Rick Karatas

More of My Scathing Emails

Writing scathing emails really helps me clear my mind and feel better when anyone has wronged me. I feel a need to tell them off. Below is another one I sent to WCB caterers (the worst) about Amerilla, the manager from hell. I have very few positive things to say about her. But let me try.

Okay, I tried, but I am not a miracle worker. Horrible human being. She tried to have me fired within the first two months she was there.

There was a captain that Amerilla was grooming to be the next best thing since sliced bread. (To reiterate: Whoever counts all the catering puns in this book and gets the correct number will win . . . absolutely nothing, but you will feel *empowered.)* This new inexperienced captain was way out of control. He didn't know what he was doing and was on a power trip. He wrote up twenty butlers at the same event once. He also got into an argument with someone who had been there for ten years about how the silverware should be placed on the table. He was wrong, but the butler still got called into the office for a meeting.

One woman who had been there forever got called in for not smiling enough. It's a wonder anyone ever smiled at all working for this company!

Anyway, Amerilla called me into the office when this doofus of a captain had written me up over something stupid. I was never sent to the principal's office in high school, but I got called into the WCB office. Amerilla told me, "One more incident and that would be the last one." I had been with this company nine years, she had been there nine minutes and she was already threatening to fire me, one of their best workers, a guy who was always on time. I'm sure it was part retaliation for the email I wrote about the understaffed event.

I finally had to write the following letter to stop the harassment. Below is the email. Some of it has been redacted (I learned how to do that from William Barr.)

Hello,

I have worked for (REDACTED) for nine years. In that time, I have never had issues or problems with any of the owners, salespeople, most captains, or butlers or ANY of the last FIVE previous General Managers. I had never been sent home from a job or written up in the hundreds of events I have worked for (REDACTED). I have given excellent service to the clients and guests, at many VIP events, and conducted myself very professionally. I believe **ALL THE CAPTAINS**, *will back me up on this, with the exception of the one captain who has the least experience, and the one I'll talk about in this letter. In all the time I have worked with (REDACTED), including at THE COMPANY OWNER'S HOUSE , until very recently I was never called into the office except once, regarding a disagreement with Morey Seamstress almost a year ago. I was* ***off the clock*** *and already signed out, at a set up event where there* **were no guests.** *(I have witnesses that I was just standing up for myself, and the other waitstaff, against Morey, who was abusing his power against the staff.) I can give the contact info of the witnesses if needed. Morey no longer works for (REDACTED), I believe partly due to the way he harassed the staff. 'This incident' is now being used against me by the current general manager, Amerilla. Since I was already off the clock, Morey was basically trying to get us to keep working, through our five hours without a half hour break, which by law he couldn't do, so I stood up* *to him. I did not curse or threaten him, I just told him he was wrong. I am being called into the office again on Oct 24th, regarding an event, but they refuse to tell me why. I asked to have a meeting with human resources first, but they said no, meet with Amerilla first. (REDACTED) from HR will be there as well.*

For the record, here is a recap of what transpired at that event:

I had a VIP table, which was EXTREMELY happy with the excellent service that was given. It was the (REDACTED) table, a new VIP client of (REDACTED), and he and his guests received very special attention from me as witnessed by (a co-owner of the caterer), who had asked that I give them special attention.

You may call both of them and ask them how the service was if you like. I got two special vegan plates from the expediter for them, and without them even asking me, I brought them fruit platters for dessert, as I knew they couldn't eat most of the ones we had. When I brought them out to them someone else asked if he could get one too. I brought one more and he was very pleased. Also, when they asked for salt and the kitchen told me there was no salt, I told another supervisor I had VIP table number two, so she told the kitchen that if he has table two, get him salt! A less experienced server would have taken the kitchen's "No" and the table would not have gotten salt. The guests at my table were wined and watered, everything bussed promptly, and they were well taken care of. They were VERY HAPPY. In other words, I did my job. This new client was very happy ***thus improving the chances of repeat business for (REDACTED) catering.***

At the staff meeting, the ***event supervisor*** *had told us* ***once the show begins we must be off the floor****. This was supposed to happen around 8:30PM. At approx. 8:20PM the lights went down and a Magic show began. My table had everything they needed. The show must have started early because at 8:20PM my table was engrossed in the show, and some of the guests at various tables asked that we move out of the way so that they could watch the show.* ***So, several waiters and myself did just that.*** *We stood out of the way of the tables, close enough in case they needed anything.* ***The other servers can testify to this.*** *That's when the captain,* ***Simon*** *(I had not seen him during service at all), ran up to the three of us and in* ***front of guests*** *started* ***yelling*** *at us to serve our tables! He was* ***belligerent****, and was basically* ***harassing*** *and* ***bullying*** *us. He was out of bounds. We tried to explain to him that our tables had everything they needed and they were trying to watch the show, but he just* ***screamed,*** *"It's not 8:30 yet, keep serving your tables!" This is not acceptable for a captain to behave like this. A* ***more experienced,*** *captain would have seen that the tables were fine or at least asked us if our tables had everything, and not try to* ***humiliate*** *and* ***badger*** *us. Two other servers were both there as witnesses, but* *we are not allowed to bring witnesses when we are called into the manager's office.*

I immediately went to the kitchen, away from guests and told one of the event supervisors, what had happened. I felt I had to, because when I was called into the General Manager Amerilla's office regarding the food and wine event, she threatened me with my job. She said that if I were involved in one more disagreement or incident with a captain that would be the last one. Even though the only other person I had an issue with in almost ten years was Morey Seamstress. I felt I couldn't chance having Simon write me up again saying I was causing problems, especially when everything had gone so smoothly with the service at my table, and the event was running fine.

What I didn't know, was that according to another captain, ***twenty other waiters,*** *had already complained about* ***Simon's abuse*** *that night, and he said he would have a talk with Simon. The other event supervisor and (REDACTED) did indeed speak with him, but we don't know what was said.* ***So, I am very confused since it seems I am the only one being called into the General Manager's office when so many others complained.***

The event itself, at least in my whole section, went well. The guests got what they needed and were satisfied. To have a ***CAPTAIN*** *approach us with an* ***outburst*** *like that,* ***berating*** *us,* ***DOES NOT IMPROVE SERVICE AT AN EVENT.*** *In fact,* ***it can hinder it.*** *Why* *the company would want to encourage* ***animosity*** *and having captains* ***antagonize*** *the staff is beyond me. This is not the only event in which the staff has had an issue with Simon. Several of the veteran workers have been written up by him and been brought into the office for the first time ever.*

My record with this caterer is very clean. It's not fair that I am being ***intimidated*** *and* ***harassed*** *by the general manager and a captain who doesn't know what he is doing. He is being allowed to abuse his power, and the butlers/waiters are afraid to file complaints for fear of losing their jobs. Yet somehow twenty butlers at this event did complain that night about Simon, which is amazing. This is not some kind of vendetta against Simon. This is not a personality conflict. In fact, I worked two events with him prior to this when he was a butler, not a captain. He asked me to help him a couple times, so I did. I believe we should all be working together, not against each other. I wasn't even going to file a written complaint against Simon since someone had a talk with him that night. But since I am being* ***SINGLED OUT****, and being* ***HARRASSED*** *into coming down to the office, which is* ***intimidating*** *and* ***stressful****, I feel I am left with no choice. Perhaps, I am being singled out and harassed in* ***RETALIATION*** *for the letter I wrote to HR a couple months ago regarding the food and wine event back in August, but I was under the impression that there is an open door policy. I was called into the office to meet* *with the general manager, about the food and wine event, which in* ***her words****, "The client wanted it understaffed." She also told the captains* ***not to put in their reports that it was understaffed.*** *The* ***SEVERE*** *understaffing and* ***conditions*** *affected the work and attitudes of the servers and captains. We were worked like plow horses in 100-degree heat, no food for seven hours in a tent that was a fire hazard. The staff wasn't even given ten minute breaks.*

I was sent home from this event because I took fifteen minutes to go downstairs to try to secure a job on my phone for the next day. I actually didn't mind being sent home for the first time in nine years, as I was about to pass out from heat exhaustion. Four or five others were sent home from this event as well, which makes a lot of sense when you are that understaffed (sarcasm). Simon, who wasn't even my captain at that event, started arguing with me when I was ***off the clock*** *and I was* ***trying to leave but I had to get the car keys from the person I carpooled with.*** *He only made the situation worse and wrote me up (which I did not know till later). I believe he said in the report I argued in front of guests. (I sent an email to the general manager to get a copy of my report, but it went unanswered). The 'discussion' we had* ***was not in front of guests.*** *It was* ***near scullery****, so unless guests were helping bus dirty plates, there were no guests around. I was just trying to get out of there.* ***(REDACTED) is a witness to that. (REDACTED) is a***

witness that I did not argue with the other captain also. *Also, I could not find a captain to let them know I needed to take a few minutes to use my phone.*

The staff should not have to feel as if we are walking on eggshells because captains are being encouraged to write up workers like a police officer with a quota to fill. And we shouldn't have to worry that at any time, a captain can write you up for whatever reason they feel like, without giving any ***verbal warning*** *or anything, especially when we are doing our jobs.* **Experienced** *captains know how to treat their staff well and get the job done at the same time. I am* **POSITIVE ALMOST EVERY SINGLE CAPTAIN,** *will back me up.* ***(REDACTED)*** *catering company is supposed to be about giving good service to the guests, and that is still what I do. I also treat the other butlers/servers well and work together with them without incident. And* ***I still enjoy working for (REDACTED) and will continue to do my best.***

We do not have to tolerate a captain that doesn't know what they are doing. It does not help repeat business for (REDACTED) either. Or tolerate one who is using their authority in an abusive way, because he knows he will be protected no matter what he does.

Please let me know when you receive this. I just want the harassment to stop. Thank you.

Sincerely,
Rick Karatas

The letter and a follow up meeting with HR did the trick to stop it, and eventually, Simon left. Rumor had it that he had a big coke problem which would explain his behavior. I never brought that up but had it in my back pocket just in case.

Jimmy, the Tyrant

Back in the day, I did many catering events together with Cara McCarty (also with her now-husband, Everett Chavez) and she told me a story about an event she had worked at Hofstra University. It was outside under a tent, and tables were set up with nice white linen. There were torrential downpours and inside the tent, the ground got wet and muddy. Cara was working tables that were way back in the corner of the tent, so that a lot of water got into that area. As she was carrying these heavy trays, she kept getting stuck in the mud. It almost came up to her mid-calves.

She went and told the guy, Jimmy, who was in charge, how challenging it was being all the way in the back and walking through the mud, and why it was taking her so long to get back to her tables. He told her to just “Shut up and get back to work.” She came up with the name “Jimmy, the Tyrant” then and there, and used it for quite some time after that.

Company Picnic

WCB caterers is cheaper than Fred Mertz. There was never a Christmas bonus, they kept most tips, the pay rate remained the same for over fifteen years, and there was no Christmas party for the staff. This from a company that makes millions and millions of dollars! They used to pay for many parking places for us when we worked an event, but then did away with that, as well. We had to park four or more blocks away from a site sometimes or pay as much as $20 for parking. Their only concern was to get that bottom line down for their stockholders. Typical corporate BS. So, not only did they not give a raise in twenty years, but they actually made it so you made less, didn't pay for breaks, and we ended up paying more for parking.

They did start doing a summer picnic for all the employees, but they were so cheap that they charged the ants that came. I'm kidding. The event was really more for their salespeople and office workers. But they got food trucks from other companies, which was a nice change, and there were games and a raffle, but no alcohol, which for me is fine, as my drinking days are over. I get drunk every **night,** but my drinking **days** are done with. That's a line that was cut out of my *Walk a Mile in My Pradas* movie, probably considered a bad dad joke, but I'm putting it here to see if the editor also cuts it out. So, if you don't see this joke, it was cut out.

The raffle was okay. They actually had a few really good prizes, most of which coincidentally went to the people who ran the office. And in fact, one of their top salespeople, who should not have even been in the drawing, won the biggest prize, which was a catered dinner at home for twelve people worth more than $1,000.

I only went to two of the picnics. At one of them, I won a small prize, which was two tickets to the Novo Theater at L.A.

Live, which costs them nothing since they have that as a venue. I could pick one singer or group that I wanted to go see within the year. I didn't even know most of the singers on the list who would be performing there. One of the few I had heard of was Bananarama. I knew like two or three of their songs, but my coworker Terry Kemp liked them and I could bring a guest, so we went together and got to see and hear them sing a song called "Cruel, Cruel Summer" courtesy of a cruel, cruel caterer.

NINE

MORE ROTTEN APPLES IN THE CATERING ORCHARD

Time to talk about some other companies that were the cream of the CRAP.

Horrible Caterers

Bratinasty Catering

WCB caterers was the worst caterer I worked for. Bratinasty Catering came in a very close second. (Neither is the real name of the company.) When I first moved to California from New York, I worked for Bratinasty for three years from 2002 to 2005. They were paying me $17 an hour. After I started working for them, I was simultaneously making $20 to $25 an hour from other caterers. They were awful to work for because they were disorganized, treated staff poorly, and did not feed you for hours.

I was always on time and did a good job. After I had worked for them for almost three years, the company was bringing in new people who didn't even know what they were doing at the same wage as me. I sent them an email asking for $18 an hour (a $1 increase per hour) since I had been there quite a while and was very reliable. They responded that I had to work fifty more events in order to get the wage bump.

I told them, "Bye, Felicia." Actually, this was like fifteen years ago, so that expression wasn't around yet. I told them to go f*#@ themselves.

Nowadays, I hear people using the expression, "You do you," which I really think is just a polite way of saying "Go f*#@ yourself." Of course, I didn't really tell them to go f*#@ themselves. I just sent a two-page letter to the owner of Bratinasty explaining why I wouldn't work there anymore. Although I'm sure he didn't read it or care, I always feel better when I get these things off my chest. I've gotten everything off my chest at one time or another, even the hair on it once or twice. Even waxing is more fun than catering sometimes.

I would not work for them again. It's about respect. Though they got me a lot of work, why would I work their parties if I were getting paid more elsewhere?

Good riddance!

After I left, there was a class action suit against Bratinasty that I should have been included in. But my former supervisors never gave my name to the law firm and I found out too late to do anything about it.

Pocomotion Events

Pocomotion Events was a company in California that I only worked for a handful of times. They were okay to a degree. And by *degree* I mean second degree because we got burned. Actually, they really weren't too bad. We were paid average there, about $20 an hour, but I only got a few jobs a year from them. One was in a billionaire's house and we didn't even get a tip. There may have been one, but we didn't see it. Did I mention it was for a billionaire?

Pocomotion is also the only company I ever really walked out on before an event even started. There was a captain named Anthony who, as soon as we arrived at this particular event, was being extremely rude to me. From the start. He was holding a cup that he was drinking out of that I knew had alcohol in it. I had worked a house party the week before with him. Not only didn't he know what he was doing, but he was drinking out of a cup at that event too, and it was also filled with alcohol. Had I not worked that event it would not have gone as smoothly. He was clueless.

Anyway, this was the second time I was hired to work with this lush. We were there about fifteen minutes and he was so disrespectful to me and talking so obnoxiously, so I figured I would leave before any parking charges kicked in. The first half hour was free.

This company only got me a few jobs a year. So sorry, but I'm not gonna take crap from a drunk captain from a company I hardly work for. I stormed up to the owner and said, "Your captain is drunk and extremely rude, and I'm not putting up with it. I'm leaving." And I did.

And it felt good. No amount of money is worth sacrificing your self-respect.

Well, maybe I would for $10K or more, but certainly not $20 an hour for a six-hour event. I was actually supposed to work the next night for them and I cancelled that. I ended up getting another job that night with someone else.

One Time Was Enough with Suriya Events

The only event I worked for them I should have walked out. The woman who owned Suriya Events Catering & Staffing Firm was one of the rudest people I've ever met. Her name was Lanoi, but I will call her *Annoy* because she was so annoying and horrible to the workers. She asked the guy that hired us for events to get him some staff for an event at a fancy Beverly Hills store. (She couldn't get her own people because no one wanted to work for her.) I even got a few people to work the event. She was rude to everyone from the moment we got there and was constantly barking orders at everyone.

Annoy was supposed to pay us that night but had some excuse when the night was over. She said she would mail the checks right out the next day. Weeks went by with no check. I had to call her several times. Then when we all got the checks we saw that she had stiffed us half an hour of pay, so I called her. She said, "Well you can come pick up the rest."

I wasn't going to waste my time and gas money. Plus, there was no tip included either. When I said she should mail us what she owed us, she said, "If you need the money that much, maybe you should get a real job." (By saying that, she insulted everyone who worked for her.) She told me on the phone that she would never use me again.

I laughed and said, "I knew within five minutes of the event that I would never want to work for you again. You're such a bitch," and I hung up.

I really *did* say that to her. I know I've been joking a lot in this book about how I told someone off, but with her I really did. Then I contacted the guy who hired us to work for her and told him never to send anyone to work for her again. I think he still sent people after that, and some didn't get paid for jobs, and they had to take her to court.

If only people would listen to me.

This was my Yelp review of her:

10/8/2017

The woman who owns this company, Lanoi Mali, was the rudest of any owners I have known in twenty years in the catering business. Worked for her only once. She treated the staff poorly, didn't pay the right amount or on time, and insulted most of the staff. The worst.

Dandy Whyzelle Catering

Another bad apple caterer in the Big Apple. (Long Island. Close enough) for which I worked many years ago had a worm as an owner. He was stoned all the time. And he wasn't just a pot smoker; he was a chain pot smoker. The guy made Willie Nelson and Snoop Dog look like amateurs.

One morning, my friend Susan Bennett was asked to get some cigarettes and a Red Bull for him, and without missing a beat she said, "Breakfast of Champions."

We worked for him in many fancy Long Island homes. These people had so much money. They would serve Cristal champagne at their parties. We would get at least $100, sometimes a $150 tip. I did work with some really cool people there, some of whom became my lifelong friends. It was just the company that left a lot to be desired.

Personally, I always got paid by them, but some other folks had trouble collecting. "Willie" owes one server thousands of dollars. A true scumbag.

Some of their clients were nice. But one I remember was awful. It was a New Year's Eve party and I don't remember all the details, but this woman was so rude that it was a horrible event to work. A couple weeks later, still fuming, I actually called her from a payphone (this was when there were payphones) and just said, "You are a bitch," on her answering machine. I didn't say who I was, but I think she may have gotten several calls like that, so it could have been anybody.

Again, I just had to get it off my chest.

Small Claims Court

I once worked for a woman in Long Island who would staff for various events. She had a habit of not paying her staff. Turned out she was an alcoholic. So, this bad apple was probably bad because she drank too many apple martinis. She was still living with her parents. (I felt so sorry for the mom.) I had called many times to try to get payment from an event, and the mom answered. You could hear the sadness in her voice. There was one event we hadn't gotten paid for, and I had called so many times that I finally filed a small claims lawsuit. She called me shortly afterwards, asking me if I had contacted one of those TV courtroom shows like *People's Court* or *Judge Judy* or something, because she got a call from them.

I hadn't, but I guess every lawsuit is public, so they had contacted her to see if she and I wanted to be on the show. She thought that since I'm an actor I just wanted to get on TV, and I contacted them. *Uhmm, no.* That's not the way I wanted to get on TV.

She ended up paying me before the small claims date. I met her on the side of an exit ramp off the L.I.E (Long Island Expressway, notice how apropos the acronym is) and she gave me the money. Probably looked like we were doing a drug deal.

That was the last time I saw her. I wonder what ever happened to her.

Chef J.R.

On the show *Dallas,* one year the big question was who shot J.R.? Well nobody shot this J.R., but I would have liked to have clocked him one. I worked for Chef J.R. in 2008 a few times. He now owns a restaurant in downtown L.A.. It always took a little while to get paid when I did a catering job for him. Then he asked me to work an event and get a crew together of six other waiters, which I did. It was an unorganized, understaffed event.

He had us get there late to save money, which didn't leave enough time for set up. Despite all that, the event went smoothly. We were supposed to get paid the next week. Almost a month later, we still weren't, and the people I brought to him kept asking where their money was. I sent him an email demanding that he pay everyone right away. He kept lying about the checks going out and always had an excuse. He replied that I was rude, and that's when I wrote this scathing email to him:

John,

You are a liar. How is that for rude? I get a whole crew to work for you, who do a great job at an understaffed event, and a MONTH LATER NONE HAVE BEEN PAID. If it were just me that didn't get paid, I wouldn't make as big a deal. In fact, every job I worked for you, you always blamed the accountant for my check coming late. But when I have others who trust my judgement in people they are going to work for, I have to say something. They all called me to ask, where are our checks? The checks didn't go out in early December like you say in your email, because you told me a week ago after a few calls and emails from me that they would go out the following morning, finally.

There's no CONFUSION. It's not like one person didn't get paid. No one was paid. I believe your last excuse was that you were in "building inspector hell." I'm sure all the waiters really care about that one. Had you just apologized for the delay and sent out the checks ASAP., it wouldn't be as big a deal, but when you come up with BULLSHIT excuses and lies, that's where I have a problem. Obviously, I won't be working for you in the future.

Signed,
A more than KINDA rude e-mail, but deserved one,
Rick Karatas

Okay Caterers

Some caterers I worked for were not great but weren't nightmares either. They didn't leave a bad taste in my mouth. (Every pun in here is intended.) While after working with some, I felt like I threw up in my mouth a little.

Thoughtless Foods

I worked for them in NYC. "Thoughtless Foods" (not their real name) were okay to work for. I think we made $17 an hour, then it went up to $20 an hour, which back then wasn't bad. They did have a great hors d'oeuvre, a mini Lamb Wellington, that was delicious. I also worked with some great people, some of whom I still keep in touch with.

At one event we worked for Thoughtless in the 1990s, the R&B group Jodeci performed. I had never heard of them, but we got a free CD even though that kind of music is not my cup of tea. If it's free, it's for me. I also got a free Gloria Estevan cassette at an HBO event when we worked for her special. As I mentioned, getting free music was a cool perk for me. Of course, this was before you could just listen on Pandora and Spotify, and other apps.

I worked quite a few events for Thoughtless, as I have for many caterers, but I don't remember many. A lot are just a blur. All of them blended together after a while. We worked on a boat for them once that went around Manhattan, which was kind of cool. This is when I found out I don't get seasick. We also worked several events at a place called Dezerland in NYC for many bar and bat mitzvahs.

Harry and the Redhead

I never saw the red head, but Harry made me see red once in a while. In fact, one time he really ticked me off. Overall a nice guy, but at one event in particular, at a temple in Long Island, he was being an obnoxious, prissy, condescending pain in my ass. It was almost the end of the event when he said something snarky and I snapped back. Then he said, "If you're going to have that kind of attitude, just keep walking," so I said, "I will," and I walked right out the door.

I will not be disrespected by anyone, especially when I am working for them. He tried not to pay the agency who sent me there, saying I left the job early. There was like fifteen minutes left of a five-hour shift, so I made sure I got my money.

Like I said, most of the time he was alright—just a dick on that day.

TEN

WEDDINGS, BAR MITZVAHS AND BIRTHDAYS, OH MY!

I've worked many of these events and the following are some that stick out in my mind, probably because they stick in my craw. I'll start with weddings.

It Never Rains in Southern California, Except When It Does

I worked a wedding in Santa Barbara, in August, when it never rains in Southern California, as the song says. I guess by never they mean 99.9 percent of the time, because this one particular day in August, Mother Nature did not get the memo.

The wedding we were working was out in the middle of nowhere. No tent, no shelter, no back up plan, a ten-minute walk to any building. We had everything set up, the tables, chairs, place settings and folded napkins on the table before the skies suddenly grew darker and darker. It started raining as the guests were arriving and the chairs were getting wet, the nice, folded napkins were getting wet. Everything and everyone was getting wet, but my sense of humor stayed dry. Everyone actually still had a good time and at least it was a warm, light rain, not a drenching rain. There was nothing anyone could do so they all made the best of it.

And I guess they say rain is good luck on your wedding day. One of the caterers I used to work for on Long Island, Fran Zaslow, used to tell us that if you stick a knife in the ground, it will prevent a rainfall. To this day, I'm not sure if that works.

Frozen Feet: The Wedding That Never Was

One of the most memorable events I worked was a (non) wedding in New York, where the groom called off the wedding that morning. The bride figured everything was paid for, so she went ahead with the party. She understood that she was better off finding out what an a-hole he was before the nuptials rather than marry him and then find out.

The bride sang a few songs with the band and really showed a lot of class. She was a good singer too. I think she sang "I Will Survive." Many guests showed up, not knowing the ceremony never took place, and most of the groom's friends and family didn't come. As I'm writing this, I became curious what percentage of weddings get called off. So, I googled it. The answer is 20 percent. The other 80 percent are foolish enough to go through with it.

Ecstasy

I worked a wedding about fifteen years ago for a caterer in California. All I remember about the event is that it was nearing midnight and we were instructed to put out a hundred bottles of water because the guests were going to be doing Ecstasy. I had never done it (still haven't), but this is when I learned that when you do Ecstasy you get dehydrated and need to drink a lot of water. Sometimes catering can be very educational.

I know many folks experience ecstasy on their honey-moons. This was the first time I found myself amid a bunch of guests experiencing ecstasy at a wedding.

At another event for this company, we served hash brownies. At one or two events where we passed brownies around, if the guests weren't taking them, I would say they were hash brownies to get rid of them faster. (I've never had hash brownies either.) I would like to say catering is my high, but as you can tell by now it is my low.

Orthodox Wedding

Years ago, in New York, I worked an Orthodox Jewish wedding. All the men stayed on one side of the room and all the women stayed on the other side. The women danced with the women and the men danced with the men. It was the first time I saw all these men with their brim hats and *payots* (sidelocks). I was reminded of this event when I watched the series *Unorthodox* on Amazon recently. The wedding scene brought back memories.

I have learned a lot about different cultures and people from catering events.

Journal Entry

I found a few old journals I used to keep. I really wish I had done more of them. This is one in which I describe a wedding I worked.

June 18, 1997

I worked a wedding this week that cost $1.2 million. That marriage better last. I made about $350. Jon Secada was at my table. He sang a few songs, not very well. Tommy Tune sang a couple of songs and so did Le Chic and Robin S. The flowers were unbelievable.

I'm glad I kept a journal once in a while. I didn't remember that event at all, and I feel bad that I said Jon Secada didn't sing well. He was at a wedding, so maybe he was drunk or had wedding cake stuck in his throat. I love the duet he did with Olivia Newton-John for the song "Every Time It Snows" on her *Christmas Wish* CD, which came out in 2007. It's beautiful.

The $5 Million Party for the Three-Year-Old Twins

You read that right. One of the parties I worked was part of a two-day event for three-year-old twins in which the parents spent $5 million or $2.5 million apiece for their kids who were too young to even remember it. Rumor had it that the family bought this huge house just for the party, and after the event, they decided they didn't like the house and knocked it down and had it rebuilt.

The theme on the day I worked was from the movie *Willy Wonka and The Chocolate Factory*. For the Willy Wonka theme day, a chocolate river was put in the yard. They even hired little people to be Oompa Loompas and run around. The tiny jars of caviar on each table were worth $50K each, and the flowers were worth well over $100K. A several-course meal was served. The three pools on the property had synchronized swimmers doing shows in them. I'm sure the champagne was not Korbel or Andre Brut. We are talking an insane amount of money spent on a children's birthday party!

The second day of the party, the day that I didn't work, was a whole other theme. From the movie *Snow White and the Seven Dwarfs.* I'm guessing they used the same little people who played the Oompa Loompas as the Seven Dwarfs, so at least those folks got two days of work out of it. I was told by a fellow employee, Frank Hinterberger, that there was a huge, real Indian elephant standing in the driveway when people arrived. Who knows, maybe they had him flown in from India?

So much money spent on three-year-olds. I'm still shaking my head in disbelief.

Look, people can do whatever they want with their money. BUT seriously, how much good could have been done with most of that money instead? They could have funded three of my scripts with that. Fed a bunch of hungry people. Cured cancer. What happened to trickle down?

Anyway, we can't say for sure these children will end up spoiled . . .

Well, yes, actually I'm pretty sure we can.

Bar Mitzvah with Oy-Fensive Music

One Bar mitzvah I worked I was appalled at the music that was being played. This music was not only inappropriate for children, but for adults as well, as far as I'm concerned. This was a party for a thirteen-year-old. Okay, yeah, these types of parties are more for the adults to show off for their friends. Every other word on every song the DJ played was either the N-word or the B-word. It was extremely offensive and degrading to women. The songs about sex were very graphic. Even scarier, the kids knew all the words and were singing along!

One of the adult guests did kind of complain to me and I agreed. One of the staff ended up sending a letter to the DJ Company complaining about the music. The caterer got mad at him for doing that. I've worked a few events where they played this kind of music and there are kids even younger than thirteen at the party.

What is wrong with people?

I have to laugh. Back when I was in high school, one of my favorite singers, Olivia Newton-John, got banned on some radio stations for her song "Physical" being too suggestive. That song was so tame compared to those we hear today. Boy, times have changed.

I have worked so many bar and bat mitzvahs that I know the playlist by heart. I know the lyrics to songs like "Hava Nagila" (which my friend in college, Joe Topale, used to sing "Have a Tequila" instead), "Cinnamon Toast and Mazel Tov."

(It wasn't really "Cinnamon Toast," but it sounded like that, and that's how me and my coworkers sang it.)

The real song title was "Siman Tov and Mazel Tov" . . . just Googled it.

ELEVEN

THE GOOD ONES

This will probably be the shortest chapter in the book. Oh alright, I actually have had the pleasure of working for some decent caterers and people. I will talk about some of my experiences with them here. To express my gratitude, but also to show that I am not the problem. After all, if I complained about every caterer I worked for, it might look like I am the problem, that there is an issue with me. While I may have more issues than *Rolling Stone* magazine and *Reader's Digest,* none of my issues with the bad caterers were unjustified.

So here are some stories from the ones I liked, and the ones who allowed me to work at a job that wasn't too bad while I was pursuing my dreams and creative endeavors, and not torturing me like other companies had done.

Serves You Right Caterers

One of my favorite companies to work for is Serves You Right, owned by Michelle Gan, located in Los Angeles, California. They treat the staff better than most of the others, they have a great clientele, and their food is really good. They usually make sure the servers sit down and get a nice staff meal within the first couple hours of the shift. Some other caterers make you wait five or six hours, then you finally just wolf something down. They are very well organized, always pay on time, and include the tip. (Again, there are some companies that illegally keep it.)

I asked Michelle some questions about her experiences as a caterer.

What was the worst catering experiences you ever had?

Working out in Malibu on a large event and the power went out. We used candles and thankfully we had a stove that used propane.

Best catering experience or funniest you had?

The privilege of cooking for President Obama. I actually thought he would eat but he didn't.

What advice would you give to someone going into catering?

You must really be a leader and have no ego.

Biggest pet peeves/most annoying things guests or staff do at an event?

Have unscheduled speeches, generally when we are trying to do the dinner service.

What are a few of the main things you would like people to know about Serves You Right?

We are a company who treats everyone the same. Everyone is a celebrity, and our job is to be of service.

The Raging Skillet

I've worked many weddings and parties for Chef Rossi in New York City. You can check out her fabulous book, *The Raging Skillet,* which became a fun Off-Broadway play as well.

From her website:

> *The Raging Skillet is one woman's story of cooking her way through some of life's biggest challenges in New York City's most unlikely kitchens. Talking her way into any cooking job she could get, a self-taught and self-made Rossi ended up owning one of the most sought-after catering companies in the city. The book features anecdotes from a life of food plus recipes ranging from pizza bagels to tuna tartare—to close each section. This tasty memoir shows us how Chef Rossi found a way to pay tribute to her roots while staying true to herself. She is definitely an original.*

The questions I asked Chef Rossi were basically the same as I asked Michelle Gan.

What was one of the worst catering experiences you ever had?

I have had some impossible kitchen situations on locations. I once had to feed 300 people from a Xerox machine closet! Lately, I am feeling old, because when I tell people that story, the millennials say, "What's a Xerox machine?" LOL

I recently catered an elaborate high-end wedding, while the sewer was backing up into the kitchen! YECH! We managed to get through it and kept all the food pristine by keeping it all on top of the table, but we had to bleach our shoes! LORDY that was not fun. Like all of the trials and tribulations we go through, the guests never knew!

Best catering experience or funniest one you had?

To this day, my favorite was when I was hired to cater the *Vagina Monologues* huge fundraiser and had to do all the food, shall we say, anatomically correct! Yep, lots and lots of edible vaginas. It's in my book of course.

Then, there's the chili story! Years ago, maybe in the late '80s, we were hired to cater a party in the Hamptons on Long Island, a cocktail party for an investor from Oklahoma, and it was important for the person who hired us to feature his Oklahoma chili.

I told him I make a great chili, that it would knock your socks off and he was like, "A Yankee girl making chili? I don't think so." I was kind of insulted. *Why couldn't I make the chili?* Anyway, he insisted on sending his chili across the country, so fifty quarts of chili were Fed Ex-ed to our New York office and we put it in the fridge.

We did all the other food. And on the day of the party, we loaded up three vans to go to the Hamptons, which were a good three hours away on a little road in the boondocks on Long Island. The chef unpacked all of the food from the truck and realized he'd left the chili back in the city. I sent someone to go to Wendy's and buy them out of all the chili they had on the premises. Then we found some ketchup and added cumin, coriander, and chili powder. We doctored it up with some other things from the fridge, topped it off with lots of cheese, and served it on the hollowed-out corn muffins that they wanted it on.

A few days later, the guy from Oklahoma calls up with his big southern accent (and I'm thinking in my head, *I'm gonna have to get my lawyer).* He asked, "Aren't you glad you used our chili? Wasn't it the best chili in the world?"

The next day our staff had Oklahoma chili as their staff meal.

What projects or events do you have coming up that you are excited about?

I am mostly excited that I finished my second book! We are looking for a publisher now! It's gonna knock your socks off. The tentative title is *Queen of the Jews.*

What advice would you give for anyone getting into catering?

Do not jump to start your own business. First, work for a lot of other caterers. Learn all the good they do, and also all the bad. The hardest part of owning a catering business, for me, is that I spend 90 percent of time on mundane and annoying business dealings. I just wanted to cook and make beautiful food displays. I was able to do that all the time when I was a chef for others. Now, as a business owner, I'm bogged down with inspectors, Con Edison inventory. BORING!

Biggest pet peeves/most annoying things guests or staff do at an event?

Here's my list.

1. NUMBER ONE, hands down, is double dipping! THERE IS A SPECIAL PLACE IN HELL FOR DOUBLE DIPPERS! The waiter has to come back to the kitchen for a new dip bowl. NO ONE ELSE GETS TO EAT! So selfish!
2. Hate the people who walk into the kitchen, while we are plating gorgeous food, with sanitary gloves on, on our table with the clean white work cloth, and they think it's okay to leave their garbage! WTF!
3. Staff talking in the kitchen is a big one. A little is okay, but there was a guy, a sweet guy, who never shut up; he would gossip about all the guests, what the bride was wearing, and so forth. It was funny for five minutes and then I need everyone to shut up. Nonstop talk is distracting.
4. Hatred of front of house/back of house. Sometimes there would be a conflict or divide between bartenders and waiters or waiters and chefs or bartenders and chefs. Just so stupid. Just get along.
5. It also bothers me that other caterers (including some I worked for in the past) didn't feed their staff enough or in a timely fashion. It was always much later than the guests had eaten, and the staff were all starving and would grab things and wolf them down off the hors

d'oeuvres tray. I always give my staff something to eat before the event so they can function.

I think I worked an event for you where the groom called off the wedding that day? The bride went ahead and had a party. Was that your event and what do you remember about it?

I will never forget that. That bride was so brave and wonderful. I went to her and asked her what she wanted to do. The money was already spent on the wedding. She said that she wanted to go ahead with it, and I told her, okay, we are gonna have the best party in the universe.

And it was! Afterwards, I sent her flowers, and wrote, "From now on when I think of bravery, I will think of you." Years later, I was telling that story to a close friend of mine and she screamed. It turned out the bride was a good pal of hers and had called her gushing about my note and flowers. The fabulous ending is that the bride found her dream hubby a year later.

The runaway groom came to her the next day begging for her to take him back, but she was NOT having it.

Natalie Sofer

Natalie is a lovely event planner in Los Angeles that I help out sometimes by supplying bartenders and staff for some house parties and charity events. She has the nicest clients and is a pleasure to work for. I asked her my questions too.

What was one of the worst catering event experiences you ever had?

I would rather not relive that experience.

Best one?

It was in 2014, a beautiful Gatsby wedding for two fantastic gentlemen. They wanted the best and I gave them the best. The timing of the day was planned and executed to the minute. We stayed authentic to the times. My clients spared no expense, from the white coats and gloves for the servers to the 1920's band, the 1927 Packard that was parked outside, and cigarette trays that held the programs which looked like old newspapers. It was one of the best weddings ever.

What advice would you give anyone thinking of getting into event planning or catering?

You need to know that this is one of the most stressful jobs ever. You have to really love what you are doing to do it. It is not for the faint of heart.

Biggest pet peeves/most annoying things guests at an event do?

A. Switching seats at the assigned tables creating a mess for all involved.

B. Drinking too much or doing coke in the bathroom. Yes, it does happen.

C. Being rude to the vendors involved.

D. Asking the pro photographers to take pictures of them with their iPhones. And on that subject, pushing photographers out of the way at the ceremony so they can take pics with their iPads.

What are a few of the main things you would like people to know about you and your company?

I give 100 percent to my clients always. They come first. What matters to them matters to me. It is first class all the way.

What awards were you up for or have won?

I have won Best of Weddings from The Knot wedding website seven times. I have won Hall of Fame from The Knot. I have won the Couples Choice Award from Wedding Wire seven times. I have been a finalist as best wedding planner in California Wedding Day four times.

Wok Star Catering/Katie Chin

Katie Chin, for whom I've only worked for a few times, is a pleasure. I always felt very comfortable, and her guests were very nice. She is the author of four cookbooks, including the award-winning best-seller *Everyday Thai Cooking*. Her most recent book, *Everyday Chinese Cookbook: 101 Delicious Recipes from My Mother's Kitchen,* was released in April 2016 as a number one new release on Amazon. The book takes into account the clients' palate preferences to produce cuisine without borders, always reflecting a pan-Asian framework that allows her to stay true to her heritage.

The questions I asked Katie were as follows.

What would you like people to know about you and your company?

Wok Star Catering specializes in modern Asian cuisine. We can handle everything from intimate dinner parties to large-scale events. Executive chef and founder, Katie Chin, is also an award-winning cookbook author known for putting her unique spin on Asian favorites and creating memorable events for her clients.

What was one of the worst catering experiences you ever had?

I was catering for a photo shoot for a magazine on a ranch. When the crew was off shooting, a bunch of cows came out of the barn and ate all the food on the table!! It was a *Playboy* shoot, so after the cows attacked my catering table, I had to serve what I could salvage to a naked lady!

(When Katie told me this, I thought to myself, *Karma will get them.* Those cows probably ended up as hamburgers—Sudi.)

Best one?

Being a featured chef at the Sundance Film Festival and having my food served to over 200 filmmakers.

What advice would you give someone getting into catering?

Keep calm and cater on! Catering is not for sissies. You have to be resilient and able to think on your toes as things are constantly moving and changing. It can also be incredibly rewarding, especially when you assemble a great team (including the author of this book, of course).

Biggest pet peeves/most annoying things guests at an event do?

Two words: double dipping.

Fran Zaslow Caterers

I worked for Fran for several years on Long Island, New York, before I moved to California. After that, Fran Zaslow Catering was sold to two guys who were always screaming at each other and also worked at a synagogue. Their act would have been great in a sitcom or reality show. But this was before reality shows were around. After they bought it, the store mysteriously burned down several years later.

When I worked for Fran, she had some wonderful people working for her, like Ellie Seidel. Ellie had been working for Fran for quite a while, and one day they discovered they had graduated high school together!

Another coworker from there was Stacy Sussman. She and I have been friends ever since. Somehow, we started saying *"Que dice?"* to each other. Neither one of us is Spanish, so I don't know why, but we still do it twenty-five years later. Stacy is a very giving person. I am very grateful for the beautiful crudité platter she made when I did a fundraiser for my movie *Walk a Mile in My Pradas*. Fran also donated some food for it, a turkey and a few other things. Stacy worked more with Fran and crew in the kitchen and remembers Fran as an excellent cook. She paid us well and was honest with tips. Her clients were nice.

Stacy told me that one year during Rosh Hashanah, the refrigeration in the store in Westbury suddenly went kaput. They had to move the whole operation for like a week or two to Fran's house in Oyster Bay, in her big back yard, and they set tables up and worked back there. Stacy now does real estate.

We worked many events at Queens College for the college president. Had some good times there. During one event at Queens College that Stacy worked, Judy Collins was a guest and Stacy was the only one working. I wasn't there for that event. Maybe Judy asked Stacy, "Where are the clowns?" and Stacy replied, "I don't know where Sudi is today."

One day Ellie came out from the kitchen and ran right into Stacy. *Boom!* Everyone laughed and I started singing (because I am the singing waiter) the Kenny Rogers-Dottie West song "Every Time Two Fools Collide."

I love to sing. I remember how one of the chefs that worked for Fran would go around singing the Hank Williams' song "There's a Tear in My Beer," and I would sometimes join in.

We worked in many people's houses and we worked a lot of Jewish holidays, like Passover, for her. We did Bernadette Peter's wedding. That was cool. At another event when Stacy worked for one of Fran's clients, the ovens in the house didn't work and it was a nightmare. They tried to use the toaster oven to heat up the hors d' oeuvres.

It was not good.

A lovely woman named Evelyn worked there, too, and was kind of Fran's right-hand man, or woman, as the case may be.

One of my favorite items from Fran was her Banana's Foster dessert. YUMMY.

I gave Fran my questionnaire to fill out.

What was one of the worst catering experiences you ever had?

When one of the drivers of one of the catering cars drove to a Scarsdale temple for a bat mitzvah and locked the keys in the car before we unloaded. We called the car owner and there was a hidden key under the fender. Whew!

Best one?

I loved my job. All were good. Once, when the host didn't tell me the right number of people and I was getting short of filet mignon, I pulled plates away from guests and then recycled the meat and re-grilled the leftovers.

What advice would you give someone getting into catering?

It requires stamina! Resiliency. Never take anything personally. Get your money before your hosts get too drunk to write a check.

"There Are Caterers, Then There's Tommy Tangs"

That was the slogan of one of the very first caterers I started working for when I moved to California. I laughed at the expression because you could really take it two different ways. It could be a good thing or a bad thing. From what I recall, they were not too bad to work for. I was only with them a year or so.

My biggest memory from Tangs is that I had to drive their van once or twice to an event—a van that had brakes that did not work very well. I was driving it down Laurel Canyon, which might have been the road that the song "The Long and Winding Road" is based on. It was very winding, and in one direction it went down a pretty steep hill.

Did I mention the brakes didn't work well? I had never driven a van before, and I was not used to driving on curving roads like this. I saw my life flash before my eyes a few times, driving to this event.

I worked with some fun people and I remember the events being okay. I think they closed down quite a few years back.

Corrine's Concepts in Catering

They were one of the first caterers I worked for on Long Island, and I remember it being a pleasant experience, though it was so long ago that I don't remember too much. Their sons worked with them and were very nice. One of them, Keith Futerman, I'm friends with on Facebook. I moved into the city, so I stopped working for them then, but they are still around after thirty-seven years. Such a very nice family to work for.

Simply Grand

I really enjoyed working for Simply Grand in NYC. Jerry Lombardi was the owner. They paid well, the parties they did were fun, and many were at Radio City Music Hall, which is an iconic space. We mostly passed food in the suite, then the guests would be given a tour. The Rockettes would show up with Santa Claus for the private Christmas parties we worked. Many kids were at these. Santa preferred the Rockettes sitting on his lap rather than the kids. I'm kidding.

Simply Grand treated their staff well. I moved to California which was a little too far to keep working for them. They eventually closed up shop and Jerry moved to another company, but I still keep in touch with him.

Favorite Personal Clients

Demetra George

I worked in the home of Demetra George, international artist and Grammy List Nominee in Classical Music, about sixteen years ago. I bartended a few of her house parties. She and her husband, Mehmet Mustafaoglu, were so nice. She loved the fact that I was half Turkish because her husband is Turkish and she is Greek. Years later, we found each other on Facebook, and she has become a good friend. She is very supportive of my creative projects.

A wonderful singer, Demetra won Miss Teenage Oklahoma City and the Miss Teenage America Talent Award at sixteen by singing "I'm the Greatest Star" from *Funny Girl*. She was Miss Oklahoma 1972 and given the U.S. Cultural Diplomacy Award for my sharing of U.S. Culture abroad by U.S. Ambassador John Koenig in 2015 while fighting breast cancer.

She has performed with over 500 orchestras and in thousands of concerts. She has sung for four American presidents, including Presidents Nixon, Ford, Carter, and Clinton.

I know there is one president she will never sing for and I don't blame her. I wouldn't either. Well, maybe some would consider my singing torture, and if that's the case, I'd be willing to belt out some tunes in front of him until I was hoarse.

Demetra also performs at many charities. In May 2015, Demetra was the guest artist for the Northern Cyprus Rotary black-tie event, "Love Makes the World Go Round," and wowed the U.S. Ambassador and the new Turkish Cypriot president. I am proud to call her a friend.

Owen and Tara Pardo

Owen and Tara Pardo, for whom I worked about twenty-five years ago, are such nice people. I worked for them for a few years a few times a year, mostly on the Jewish holidays and quite a few Thanksgivings when they lived in New York and continued when they moved to New Jersey. When I moved to California, it became too big a schlepp—although they would have been worth the trip. They made me feel like family. Their guests were all wonderful as well. I have remained friends with them, mostly on Facebook.

People like that were great. If they were all like that, this book would not exist. I worked for Tara's lovely parents as well, Dr. Ira Sacker and his wife Marianne. Dr. Sacker specializes in eating disorders and cowrote the wonderful books, *Dying to Be Thin: Understanding and Defeating Anorexia Nervosa and Bulimia—A Practical Lifesaving Guide* and *Regaining Your Self: Understanding and Conquering the Eating Disorder Identity.* He's been on *Oprah, The View, Good Morning America,* CNN, MSNBC, and many other programs and stations.

Mona and Wayne Engel

I worked a couple of New Year's Eve parties for them. Such nice people. Stacy Sussman referred me to them. I keep in touch with Mona, but sadly, Wayne passed away a few years ago. I was so honored when they both attended the film festival screening in New Jersey in 2011 for my film *Walk a Mile in My Pradas*. They drove all the way from Long Island.

Mona also came to my book signing with Stacy for *Rainbow Relatives* at the store Book Revue in Huntington, Long Island, which I so appreciated. I didn't mind working New Year's Eve for people like that. It was a good way to bring in the New Year.

Marci Valner

Definitely one of my nicest clients. I always felt welcome in her home. She and her husband, Rudy, were so nice to work for and their guests were lovely also. Rudy liked to make drinks for the guests, which made my job easier. Marci is a great cook and makes the food herself for her house parties. She's organized, which makes it easier to serve her guests more efficiently. Her special dessert, a Pavlova, a meringue with fruit on top of it, is to die for. I worked a Thanksgiving or two at her house. I don't mind working on a holiday for people like that.

Sam and Ashan Leslie

I have been honored to work for these guys, a married couple in Hollywood whom I now think of as my good friends. Several years in a row on behalf of Natalie Sofer, I worked and staffed butlers and bartenders for their annual fundraising event, the Laurel Foundation Toy Drive and Fundraiser, at their lovely home. About 200 people came each year and donated to the cause, including bringing toys for kids. There was an auction where even more money was raised. The mission of the Laurel Foundation is to empower children, youth, and families affected by HIV/AIDS. Many transgender and at-risk youth are served by them through educational and support programs offered in a safe and trusting environment.

Mrs. Altheim

It was still in my early catering days on Long Island. Mrs. Altheim was very nice. I always liked the music she played, like Linda Ronstadt's *What's New* album, when that came out—which reminds me that I worked in Nelson Riddle's daughter's house once as well. Mrs. Altheim always helped put things away at the end, even though she had enough money to have a housekeeper do it. She also tipped well, like $100. I worked quite a few house parties for her over several years before I moved into the city.

I actually changed my first flat tire at the Altheims' house. I had worked seven hours and came out to find that my car tire was flat. I had never changed a tire before, as it was the first car I owned. I don't think I even knew about AAA back then. So, here I am in a tuxedo (I suppose I took the jacket off), getting dirt on me.

Though I had no clue how to change a tire, I had seen Lucy and Ethel do it on *I Love Lucy* once. Actually, I think I was with a friend who had to change his tire a short time before that. I just tried to remember what he did.

Anyway, I did it. Mrs. Altheim's husband thought I was crazy, like, "Why don't you just call someone and pay them to do it?" He didn't know that my budget was tighter than Olivia Newton-John's pants in *Grease*.

A Few Other Great Clients

Paul Lerner and Stephen Reis—I bartended a few Oscar parties and summer parties at their house. They were so nice and so were their guests. I even knew a few of the guests who would come. One time I ran into Paul and Steve at an Erasure concert at the Wiltern Theatre in Los Angeles, which was a fun concert.

When I lived in New York City, another woman I worked for, who was very nice as well, was Trish Metz—always a pleasure. Her husband was very nice.

Also Mrs. Kaltman, a lovely woman on Long Island whose husband was also very nice. He loved music as much as I did, and I think he may have been in the industry. We had some nice conversations. I worked some cool summer barbecues in their backyard.

There is such a difference in these kind of great clients who treat you well, as opposed to those who don't. There really are more good ones than bad ones, but these few really stand out.

TWELVE

EVENTFUL EVENTS

Some of the catering jobs I did over the years really stick out in my mind, some good, some bad.

Montana

One of the best events I ever worked in catering was when the caterer flew us to Montana to work a party in honor of the CEO of a rather famous investment company for his seventieth birthday. They put us up in a hotel. Most of the staff had to share rooms, but I lucked out and got my own somehow.

The first day we got there, we had the afternoon off. It was almost 100 degrees, so a group of us went to the river and swam. The view was beautiful; we could see snow on the mountain from the river. Later, the sunset was beautiful. Now I know what the John Denver song "Wild Montana Skies" means. I looked at three different locations in the sky and saw three totally different breathtaking sights. One side had a beautiful sunset. On another I saw a few stars. Lightning was flashing in a third corner of the sky.

That evening, we went to the festival in town in Missoula. It was a beer fest or something like it, and there were bands playing. It was fun.

On the second day, we did set up for the event.

The third day was the day of the event. We changed and showered in the fancy country club. Stevie Wonder and Huey Lewis sang at the birthday party.

For my own seventieth birthday party, I'm going to ask Dolly Parton to sing.

Huey was actually in an elevator at some point and we saw that he was dressed in jeans and a white dress shirt, which is what our uniform was for this event, and he said something like, "Look. I'm dressed like the help." I remember one of the workers later said he was offended by that remark, but I don't think Huey meant anything disrespectful. I think his "Heart of Rock & Roll" was in the right place.

We were paid really well and got a decent tip. Again, another catering job that did *not* suck the life right out of me.

It is a curse and a blessing to work those kind of jobs because they kind of suck you into continuing to cater when you should be pursuing your passion and dream. If they were all really bad experiences, it would be easier to quit. When I did really awful events, it was incentive for me to concentrate more on my creative endeavors.

The Oscars

I've worked many Oscar parties. Does that sound exciting and glamorous? It's not. For a few years, I worked inside the ballroom at the Kodak (now the Dolby) Theatre in Hollywood. Yes, a lot of famous actors were walking around holding their heavy statues. They barely sat down to eat, and then they swooped off to private events. It was a little stressful, mostly because the caterer made it stressful. You could be there till 3:00 or 4:00 AM, which is way after my usual bedtime.

After a few years of working them, I requested to do the crew feed, which was much easier. It was in a separate building and we were just serving those who helped in setting up the event. This included the lighting and sound people, those who decorated the room and the sets, and writers like Bruce Vilanch, who wrote the jokes for the show for many years. Working the crew feed was much more laid back and with better hours; sometimes we worked from just 9 AM to 5 PM.

Then, I really smartened up and requested a job from 7AM to 1 PM doing nothing but handing out parking passes in my jeans, sneakers, and sweatshirt to all the unfortunate other servers working the event in the ballroom!

For the chefs, it's a lot of work to do an event like the Oscars, but at least they don't have to deal with the chaos on the floor. One of my favorite chefs, Keith Johnson, said, "I had some of my best catering experiences working the Oscars, every year, from prep all the way to execution. It's amazing to see from start to finish how everything comes together. It's a lot of hard work from all the chefs and staff."

Pajama Party

About twelve years ago, I worked an event in a house with a pajama party theme, where everyone, even the staff, wore pajamas. We were given a brand-new pair of pajamas to wear and keep. I still have them. They've lasted so long because I usually sleep in the buff.

I know. TMI.

If I had pictures in this book, I would put in that one (not of me in the buff, but me in the pajamas). At the event, my job was standing behind a buffet in my pajamas. I only fell asleep twice, but it fit the theme of the party.

The stupid thing at this event was that the caterer had us wear our normal black shoes with the pajamas–not slippers or sneakers, but uncomfortable black shoes. Sometimes the bosses do not use common sense at catering jobs; and when I say *sometimes,* I mean *75 percent of the time.*

The *Sideways* Premiere

One of the caterers I worked for did a lot of movie premieres. I remember one, in particular, for the film *Sideways,* starring Virginia Madsen and Paul Giamatti. I later saw the film, which I really enjoyed. The premiere went all out with catering. Full premium bars, bountiful buffets, and really good passed hors d'oeuvres. The guests were having a great time and loved the movie. I remember thinking it was one of the best premieres I ever worked. I wished I could have been a guest instead.

About a week later, I was going through my emails I had fallen behind on, and there were hundreds. I came upon one from SAG where I was invited to the *Sideways* premiere. The email was dated before I had accepted the shift to do the catering job, so, in fact, I could have gone as a guest. This was a lesson for me to check my emails more often, so I don't miss an opportunity like that again.

Anyway, enough of me WINE-ing over not seeing the movie *Sideways* as a guest.

Another Journal Entry

I came across this journal entry while cleaning out the attic.

May 13, 1997

Last night I worked till almost midnight at the 21 club. It was for the opening of the movie Night Falls in Manhattan. There were quite a few stars there, like Armand Assante, Montel Williams, and Richard Dreyfuss. There were some rude guests there, not that bad. Just impatient people. I don't have the patience for impatient guests. I have a LOW tolerance for HIGH-maintenance people. I also worked an eighty-fifth birthday party at the 21 Club this week.

9/11

On September 11, 2001, I was working a catering gig at Hugo Boss in New York City for Fashion Week through Table Tales catering. The location of the branch was on Eleventh

Avenue near Twenty-third Street and we were on the eleventh floor. I was putting out the bagels and coffee and such at the breakfast food station when, all of a sudden, some of the Hugo Boss workers were kind of running into one of the other rooms in a hurry. Something was going on. But there were no windows in the room I was in, so I didn't know what.

I could hear a commotion from the room they all rushed toward. I thought it must be some kind of "fashion emergency." It had poured the night before, so I thought maybe there was a leak, and something got wet and ruined, which is a huge catastrophe in the fashion industry. I would find out shortly that the emergency was a lot more serious than I ever would've guessed.

Finally, my curiosity got the best of me and I ventured into the other room. Everyone was looking out the window, I said, "What's going on?" They said a plane had gone into the World Trade Center. I looked and saw some smoke coming out of the building in the distance. At that time, I thought it was one of those small planes with just a pilot. Anyway, I had work to do so I went back into the other room and made sure everything was okay on the breakfast station.

A short while later, I heard huge gasps and screams coming from the other room. I immediately went in there and now we could see smoke coming out of both buildings. They had just witnessed the second building getting hit. I knew right then that this was a terrorist attack.

One of the workers there said, "There must be something wrong with the control tower." I thought to myself, *That's just stupid, the pilots can see big, huge buildings in front of them.*

Anyway, I didn't want to get in trouble. I felt I should get back to my duties. As more news unfolded, it became clear something really dangerous was happening. The person in charge of the event asked me if I minded staying to keep doing what I was doing. They said I should call anyone I needed to call to tell them I was okay. This was okay with me as I actually felt safer there than going outside in the streets. So, I stayed and mostly watched the giant TV that was on in the office, showing the nightmare unfold.

Then it happened. The first tower collapsed completely. I think my jaw stayed wide open for fifteen minutes. A short while after this, one of the people in charge of the event came up to me. She asked if I could call the caterer and ask them if they could bring a few extra sandwiches when they brought the lunch as some people were now stuck in the building and they could use the extra food.

Now, mind you, everything was closing down in the city, including the streets, and there were sirens going off. I knew it would be impossible for the caterer to even make the delivery they were originally supposed to. I tried to tell the woman who asked me to call the caterer, but she insisted I call, so I did. Oh, and by the way, the caterer was located downtown on Water Street very close to where the Twin Towers were.

Steven Smith the owner answered, and I said, "The lady here wants to know if you can bring some extra sandwiches for the lunch." I felt like an idiot asking this because he knew I knew that it was impossible. His response was, "Tell her to go f*#@ herself."

I found out later (or maybe he told me then) that as I was asking him that question, people were coming into his catering office covered in soot and dust. Some had blood on them from escaping the falling building debris.

So anyway, I told the lady what Steve said, to go f#@* herself. Not really. I don't remember exactly what I said. Maybe something like, "Don't hold your breath."

They had asked me to stay until about 1 PM so that's when I left. I was able to get a bus across town, but buses weren't running downtown, so I had to walk about fourteen blocks home. It was surreal. Soldiers were in the streets.

It was eerily calm and quiet, but I could still hear "Tell her to go f*#@ herself in my head, and I chuckled to myself.

Fundraisers

"We were going to try to cure cancer but decided to have a party instead."

That's a quote from my coworker Krysta Florzyk. The amount of money spent on fundraisers is crazy. If they took all the money spent on these parties and used it toward curing diseases, they might be able to cure the actual diseases.

I've worked many fundraisers. The following are just a few I remember.

Charity for Hospital

Set up for this event was very complicated. Must have cost a fortune with the matching china and flowers. I get it. You want the folks who gave all that money to have a good time and feel they got something out of the money, but after a while these things seem more for show.

This particular event was for a good cause. Jimmy Kimmel was helping to raise money for a hospital where they had saved his son's life. He was the MC and was very emotional. The entertainment was the Kung Foo Fighters, who sang, and the performer Pharrell, who I think lip-synced. A little girl, maybe eight years old, who I think was a patient, came up on stage and danced and sang with him to his hit song "Happy." It was very cute.

Dan Levy from the show *Schitt's Creek* was seated at my table. I love that show. It's really funny. I wanted to tell him how much I liked the show, but I didn't. I guess I didn't want to talk Schitt when I'm catering, I already feel like it.

American Heart Association

One company I worked for did a big outdoor fundraiser every year for the American Heart Association, and our staff meal for this event was McDonald's. What is wrong with this picture?

To be fair, this wasn't the American Heart Association's fault. The caterer ordered it for us. I believe the food served to the guests was very healthy—once again proving how little this particular catering company, ("WCB caterers") cared about their own staff.

Clooney and Clinton

George Clooney hosted a fundraiser at his house for Hillary Clinton when she was running for president. I left seven of my scripts on his doorstep before I left. I'm kidding. I left six.

Okay, we, of course, would not be allowed to do something like that (though if he had liked one of my scripts, and then produced or starred in one of them, it would have been worth getting fired from catering, now wouldn't it?)

The folks at my table didn't seem too impressed and left before it was even over, and I'm guessing they paid a pretty penny to be there.

The No-Knives-Out Bush Fundraiser

I worked a fundraiser for a George W. Bush event. I'm not proud of it, but we normally don't know until we get there who or what the event is for. We had to wait outside the house for like an hour while dogs sniffed the premises for bombs. The event was easy to work. We all had to leave the floor when Bush spoke, so we never even saw him, but what I remember most about the event was that no knives were allowed on the table. Not just steak knives. Any kind of knife, even butter knives were not allowed. Maybe not even plastic knives.

Emmy Party

I worked an Emmy party about fifteen years ago. What made this really suck was that two days earlier I had attended the pre-Emmy party as a guest, thanks to my friend Scott Buford who is the senior creative director for them. So, Friday

I was a guest amongst all these stars who were nominated, hanging out and having fun, and then, on Sunday, I was asking them "May I take that plate?"

What a difference a day or two makes.

THIRTEEN

FLUSTERCUCKS

HORROR STORIES FROM FRIENDS

Ironic that I'm putting my friend's horror stories in chapter 13. I asked them some of their most horrific events to share here and will include a few of my own.

Susan Bennett is a very good friend of mine. I catered with her twenty-five or thirty years ago and we have remained good friends. We would crack each other up at our events and I have many fond memories of working with her. I moved to California in 2002, but I visited her a few years back when I was on the East Coast. She said, "Stop by, but all I have to offer are bagels and cream cheese." She had me at *bagels.* Long Island bagels are the best!

I lived for two years in Long Beach, Long Island, with Mike McCutcheon and Mark Kasper, both of whom I am still friends with, across from a twenty-four-hour bagel joint and gained ten pounds. Man, how I've missed Long Island/New York bagels since living in California. They just aren't as good anywhere else! (I think I ate six while I was at Susan's house visiting). It was great to see her and catch up with her, so I called her when I was writing this book, asking her for her best story about her worst catering nightmare. She had so many it was hard to pick just one. This is the gem she came up with.

You've Got Chocolate on My Mercedes by Susan Bennett

It was February of 2006 on Long Island. A Mercedes Benz event where repeat customers were invited to the dealership. My staff, including my daughter, Jessi, at her very first catering event, was there to serve complementary beverages and food. They gave us a list of rules of what we could and couldn't do, because it was a dealership. My crew could only come in a certain entrance because they didn't want the equipment we were bringing in to damage anything.

There was a chocolate fountain display that I immediately questioned at the meeting. It was on a serpentine half - moon table, with different fruits on it, like bananas and strawberries on skewers, set up on this beautiful table right across from the bar. Everything was going well at first. We loaded in all the equipment through the back so we wouldn't hit the cars. Then, in setting up the display, as we were putting up the chaffing dishes, it was discovered that these rented dishes still had food in them from another job. Now we had to find somewhere to wash these out. There was no kitchen really, but there was a hose in the parking lot and that would have to do.

Everyone could see us outside, and did I mention this was February on Long Island? Not exactly a warm beach day. We had to heat up the food outside under a tent. I don't think the dealership expected what was happening. Plus, many of the invited guests had brought their children to the event. Neighbors of guests came, there were families of twelve, it seemed like everyone and their uncle showed up. Children were running around ignoring all the gold ropes around the models of cars, my wait staff, however, had to walk around these.

At this point, the party was not going well. Halfway through, it was pointed out to me by the manager that the chef hats were not being worn, as if this was our only problem. I passed the message on to the cooks who basically told me to go have sex with myself. I laughed it off as I knew it was a stressful day.

Then it happened. It was Armageddon. We had been working several hours and finally I walked up to the bar and said, "Pour me a beer or I'm going to kill someone." As the bartender was pouring my beer, he had a look of fright and horror come upon his face. It sounded like slow motion to me when he screamed out, "Oh nooooooo!!!" I quickly turned around and there goes the chocolate fountain. The whole table collapsed because children were leaning on it and jumping on it trying to put their fingers in the chocolate.

Now there was chocolate everywhere. Willy Wonka would have been proud. People were screaming. I was screaming the loudest 'cause I hadn't even had one sip of the beer yet.

After the table came down with all the chocolate, the kids just jumped right in. The parents never left the buffet line where they were now packing food up in paper towels and napkins to take home. The manager came up to me. The manager started screaming at me, as if it were me who pulled the table down, when, in fact, it was these little bastards that were allowed by their parents to run amuck. Meanwhile, the chef behind the buffet just stood there when all this was going on.

Kids were now crawling through the chocolate, picking up the fruit off the floor, running around touching everything with their chocolate-covered hands. The golden ropes that were "protecting" the Mercedes cars were no longer gold. They were golden brown. Now there was chocolate on many a Mercedes because children can go under ropes. Everyone was screaming as the party came to a halt.

To clean up, I had to send someone to Home Depot to get us buckets and a mop. Meanwhile, most of my staff had left. So, it was pretty much just me and my executive chef doing the cleaning. We didn't clean out the chaffing dishes from the rental company. In fact, we sent it back with food in it since they delivered it with leftover food in it from a previous event.

I didn't have a cell phone back then. If I did, and could have put the whole fiasco on video, I'm telling you it would have gone viral.

The thing that irked me the most was that these Mercedes people sent all these rules that we, the caterers, my waitstaff, had to follow, such as not touching anything. But they didn't even think about the people that were going to come to the event.

That's what happens when you say, "Free liquor and food." You get riffraff showing up.

Why did they have to have a chocolate fountain? I questioned that from the beginning, mostly because:

A. I hate setting them up.

B. This kind of a catastrophe is bound to happen.

Not Just Blowin' Smoke by Francesca Alexander

Another woman I worked with and have remained good friends with relayed the following story to me about one of her worst experiences in catering. In her words . . .

I was sent to work at a penthouse suite, one I had worked at before and didn't want to go back to. No one who ever worked there wanted to go back. The space was a pain to work in, the work was hard, and the host did not tip. I told the people I work for not to send me there again, but somehow I was there for a second time.

When we got there, the guests were not there yet. They were going first to a reception at an art gallery and then would come back to the penthouse for a sit-down meal.

A fire had broken out in the building and the whole building was filling up with smoke and so was the Penthouse. We could not get out, the hallway had filled up with smoke, and we were told to stay put, from the front desk. We could see the firetrucks outside. Thank God one of the waiters had the sense to wet some towels and put them under the door.

I had what you might say was an epiphany as I thought, *Oh no. Am I really going to go out like this? In a fire, wearing this dreaded Penguin outfit* (tuxedo), *is this how I will be remembered? You've got to be kidding.*

Eventually the fire was put out. Some chemicals had caught fire a few floors below. The party went on as scheduled, we worked our asses off . . . and still no tip.

This near-death experience propelled me to take more action towards what I really wanted to do with my life (which didn't really include catering) and to not second-guess myself on that, and to start training for things I really wanted to do. I told myself, *This is what I am committed to do from now on!*

And I wasn't just blowin' smoke! Pun intended. I did follow through.

Charmaine Broad's Off-Broadway Story . . . The Show Must Go On

This story comes from my friend Charmaine, whom I worked with at the Raging Skillet. In her words . . .

We were doing a wedding for a lovely couple. She was an actress (and gorgeous) and he was something, I think an actor. It was a Friday night wedding at the Green Building. Anyway, we were setting up and the bride comes in. She was an understudy in an Off-Broadway play. She was a bit upset. The star of the show was deathly sick and couldn't go on. She had explained to her producers that she was getting married, so it would be impossible to fill in.

Well, you know the story, the show must go on. It did! The show was 8PM, so they had to leave Brooklyn no later than 7PM to get there on time. They had the lovely ceremony and left with loads of fanfare. All the guests stood on either side of a row and cheered them out. They hopped in an Uber and I'm sure made out like crazy on the way to Manhattan. They made it to the theater on time.

We packed up loads of hors d'oeuvres for them. The show was a huge success and then they came back and danced and partied their formal wear off. It was lovely and all were sooo happy and thrilled to be there.

I saw my friend in a play a couple months ago and she showed me the cast list. On it was the bride! I even remembered her name! It was lovely!! It was magical and made the *New York Times.*

If It Weren't for the Last Minute

Another stressful story Charmaine told me. Her words . . .

I was working with a party planner at Studio 450. The bride and groom were from the other side of the world, so we had taken care of everything beforehand, with the Great Party Planner. The venue insisted I use their own rental company. I balked repeatedly, but they insisted. The day of the wedding, the rentals were supposed to be one of the earliest pieces to arrive. The party planner called to find out what the hold-up was and got no answer. This went on forever! I called, she called still no answer. No anything!

Studio 450 is a raw space that has absolutely no furniture or anything. We were doing a wedding in less than two hours for 200 people and were still without a bar, tables, chairs, or any kitchen proofers, trays, or oven—NOTHING!! The time was a-tickin' and still no rental company. WTF? The people at Studio 450 said they had some things. Something that could be used as a bar and a couple of chairs. I sent someone out to get plastic cups.

Thanks be to Jesus we already had booze and mixers. I had ordered those from RELIABLE sources. The bride and groom arrived with their enormous family, but were in the wedding space outside, upstairs. We kept the downstairs closed off. There was nothing in there!

Now, guests would be arriving in half an hour. FINALLY the SOBs showed up! I had all the waiters go to the rental truck. They brought up all the chairs, tables, and glassware for upstairs. The couple knew nothing!! Wow!!!

We asked the rental company, "What happened?" and they said they had a FIRE. "Then why wouldn't you call us as we called you many, many times?" No answer on that one. And we come to find out later, the fire was two weeks beforehand. Bloody asshats!

The party planner got them to refund the couple half the bill. She worked her buns off for that. Never did she get tipped. Nor did any of us. Goes to show you. Yipes, MoFkers!!

After that, one of my best waiters refused to work with us anymore. Hey, it wasn't my fault. Also, for an event after that, someone wanted to save money, and they found this really inexpensive rental company. Would I mind using that one?

I told them what happened before with the other company and told them the reason I use mine. It may be a bit more expensive, but at least I know they'll show. All this for a buck.

Kim Kadel's Catering Nightmares

I used to work a lot with Kim in New York. Here is her horror story, which she calls "Lost in Jersey." This is my interpretation of what she told me.

Kim worked for a company in NYC, with which I worked also. She drove with a guy, who would be working one event with her, and on the way there they were supposed to drop off a coworker at a different house for another event. She called this guy "Baby Bokchoy" because he was a big baby and Asian. Yes, we know it's not politically correct, but this was twenty years ago.

Anyway, the event Baby Bokchoy was working was about fifteen minutes away from the event Kim was working in. A house that was hard to find. There was no WAZE or Map Quest back then. They finally found it, dropped him off, and went and worked their event. Over the next couple of hours, her coworker proceeded in getting totally annihilated on the job—drunk as a skunk. He was loud and belligerent in the kitchen and didn't care about anything.

They got done with their event and now they had to go pick up Baby Bokchoy from his event. It was now dark, and even harder to find the house, and the drunk guy she worked with had lost the paper with the address on it, so he was of no help. Then the drunk guy had to pee really bad and made her stop. He peed on the side of the road and got some on her tire.

They were driving in circles in Jersey for over an hour when miraculously they found the house. But they were so late that by the time they got there Baby Bokchoy was no longer there. The people had kicked him out of the house. Kim didn't know how long he'd waited outside on these people's steps before he gave up and left, but he was gone.

Kim and her intoxicated coworker drove around a while more looking for him but never found him. As I said, there were no cell phones back then. Later, they found out he had left the property and was walking down a road in his black uniform and hoodie with a backpack on his back. The police had picked him up, asking what he was doing roaming around late at night like that. He must have looked suspicious and someone called the cops on him.

The guy also stutters, so I'm sure that didn't help his case any.

The American Music Award Fiasco

I once worked for a caterer that was hired to serve 5,000 people at an American Music Awards event. It was a disaster, as I could have foretold. I was the buffet attendant and would be calling for whatever food items I was running low on. But the food just was not coming and all the other buffets were having the same problem with the kitchen. Most of us were out of every item for like half an hour with dozens of guests waiting in line. We servers were stuck behind the buffets looking like we didn't know how to do our jobs because there was no food.

Somehow I think the caterer was hired again the next year, despite the fiasco.

JoAnna's Worst Catering Story

My good friend, JoAnna Frohn, who used to do staffing in New York for various caterers, mentioned that when she first started staffing for catering the industry was very sexist. An event would need fifty waitstaff and only two of the servers would be women, and they would usually be assigned to coat check. The women were treated much worse than the men. They were treated like crap yet worked as hard as the guys, but still got no respect. She says it's gotten better since women rose up and many now are coordinating and running events.

One of JoAnna's worst catering experiences was when she worked a wedding, and the caterer was mad and jealous that the bride liked JoAnna better than her. She said to JoAnna at one point, "At least the groom liked me." On top of that, the caterer messed up the whole event with the schedule. JoAnna had the staff presetting the salad, but the caterer decided to extend the cocktail hour another hour without telling her. The caterer made it so hard for JoAnna to do her job, and then the bride took it out on her because everything was off. The bride later apologized, saying, "I'm sorry I was curt with you," and JoAnna graciously told her she didn't need to apologize or to feel bad for what the caterer did wrong.

You Can't Have Your Cake and Hear Judy Collins Too

JoAnna and I were working in the kitchen at an event once, cutting up the cake to go out. This was taking a while and we were already late getting it out. From the kitchen, we could hear the band and I thought the singer sounded like Judy Collins. I said, "It sounds like Judy Collins is singing," and Joanna said, "I don't care who the f&^% is singing, we need to get the cake out!"

I could never listen to Judy Collins the same again, but I have looked at cake from both sides now.

Don't Burn the Bacon

Chef Keith Johnson told me about the worst catering experience he ever had. He was with Wolfgang Puck working at an event in the Geffen Contemporary at the MOCA in Downtown Los Angeles. Chef Wolf was a guest and Chef Adam Del Bado was the chef for the event. Keith burned the bacon for one of the dishes with no idea how to recover it!

Fortunately, Chef Matt and Chef Adam did. I'm assuming they passed it off as a Cajun dish.

By the way, I love bacon. In fact, if there's no bacon in heaven, I may not want to go.

Recycled Ravioli

Chef Marcos Rodriguez, with whom I worked several events, told me his worst catering experience. It was his very first large-scale event for 300 guests and his very first executive chef position. It was also for a very prominent Hollywood executive who was throwing a wedding for his daughter at his large estate in the Santa Barbara area. The client had even built a barn on his vast property for the event. The whole thing cost well beyond seven figures.

Marcos said he had to prove himself in two very huge ways, as a leader and as someone who could produce a high caliber of food. For a whole week, he was dotting all Is and crossing all Ts, and would go over the counts and measurements with his sous chefs, over and over and over.

Well, it all began really, really well and was just flowing perfectly until they were on to the second course, the ravioli with sauce, garnish and all. It all came to a halt when, at plate 150, they ran out of raviolis. Thankfully, the event was so large that they decided to start collecting plates from the first guests who were served, including the hosts of the wedding, and no one was the wiser that they were getting unused portions compliment of the other guests.

I thank Marcos for sharing that story. Truthfully, that kind of recycling food at events happens a little too often.

FOURTEEN

THERE ARE NO HOLIDAYS FOR CATERERS

If you cater, chances are you give up many holidays to work at house parties or events. This applies to weekends as well. Your day off is Monday. Most people hate Mondays. People in the foodservice industry love Mondays.

I've worked many New Year's Eves, and the good thing about that is starting the year off making some moolah. I remember coming in really late from one New Year's Eve event on Long Island many years ago. It was probably three or four in the morning. I was exhausted and sore all over. I got into the bathtub, which felt great, and I remember thinking, *This is the last time I will work on New Year's Eve.* Guess what? I never did it again.

Okay, so I did. Bite me (another catering pun).

The money is good on New Year's Eve.

Watching the Ball Drop from Inside

One New Year's Eve, I bartended an event in an apartment that overlooked Times Square. I was nice and warm inside and could see everything outside. I was making a few bucks without freezing my butt off, unlike everyone outside who watched the ball drop while their balls froze. I also had easy access to a restroom, which I'm sure those thousands of people all squished together outside did not.

A woman came up to the bar, and we both seemed familiar to each other, but neither of us could place it. Turned out, we graduated high school together. Still, it had been over ten years, and we both were going by different names, which was part of the reason for our confusion. My legal name is Sudi, but I was going by Rick for acting, and she had changed her name too. Once we said our real names, we remembered right away.

She was a very nice, sweet woman, and it was good to see her. However, her husband was a bit of a jerk. I think he was a doctor who believed he was superior and important. When he heard I do some acting, he said, "So, what do you want to be when you grow up?"

I just said, "I'm okay doing what I'm doing."

I think my old friend was a little embarrassed by his rude behavior. As they were leaving, she gave me a kiss on the cheek and wished me luck with everything. She was very sweet, and hopefully, that pissed off her worse half.

Y2K Madness

As the end of 1999 was approaching and New Year's Eve was coming up, I guess they were having a hard time finding people to work. Most caterers were offering $100–$125 an hour, which was pretty much double what it normally would be for a holiday rate. I was signed up to work for "Thoughtless Foods" for $125 an hour, but the party got canceled less than a week before the date due to a death in the family. (Like that's a good excuse?) They did pay us $125 for the inconvenience. I ended up picking up another shift from Fran Zaslow's catering company to work a house party for $100-an-hour cash (which, of course, I claimed, if anyone from the IRS asks. If no one asks, well . . .).

My partner, Carlos, and a chef worked that night. And I use the word *worked* loosely. All we had to do was serve some hors d'oeuvres to fourteen guests for a few hours, and then serve champagne at midnight. It was the easiest $700 I ever made in one night (from catering anyway, LOL). Plus, I got paid the $125 from the other canceled party.

Of course, we all had some champagne. So, this was not a gig that sucked the life right out of me. In fact, it actually breathed a little life into me. A great way to bring in a new decade!

Other New Year's Eves

I found one of my journals (wish I kept more of them) recently from January 1995. The first paragraph I wrote reads:

Started off the New Year bartending a party in Long Beach five minutes from where I live. I made $220 cash. Half the crowd was straight, and half was gay. They played some Abba songs that I used to love as a kid. Very nostalgic.

July Fourth with the Event Group

I worked on occasion for the Event Group owned by Ellen Federico for a few years. They did all kinds of different and fun events. A lovely woman, Valerie McCaffrey, worked with them as well. I made her laugh once (maybe more than once), but I was carrying this huge tree plant that was a decoration for the room and so big it covered my whole face. She asked if I was okay, and I said, "Yeah, but I can't see the forest through the tree." She still remembers that.

I worked for Event Group when I lived in NYC, and one event I remember was July Fourth by the Hudson River for the boat parade. All we had to do was collect tickets from people entering for holiday pay of $40 an hour. Danny DeVito and Rhea Pearlman handed me tickets. (This is before I was writing scripts. Otherwise, who knows, I may have handed them one!)

I also remember that we saw a naked person, curtains and blinds wide open, on the tenth floor of a nearby building. Well, July Fourth is about freedom, and this guy was free as a bird. This job was definitely on my list of top five easiest jobs.

We did some fun Christmas parties for the Event Group as well—doing tasks like handing out treats to kids and stockings full of candy, we got to take home the leftovers with all the extra candy. My dentist loved these jobs.

Halloween

Speaking of candy, I bartended a party in the 1990s on Halloween. The guests were all going to be coming in costume. We were all in uniform, the "penguin look," full tuxedo. So, I jokingly said we should be in costumes too. We bartenders could be Chippendales dancers. We just needed to lose the tux jacket and shirt and keep the bow tie on. The caterer loved the idea, and next thing I knew, me, being Turkish, and the other bartender, who was Greek, wore only black pants and a bowtie. I'm not sure if being shirtless increased our tips or decreased them, but I was in my mid to late twenties and in pretty good shape.

Christmas Time

The busiest time of the year for everyone, the holiday season, is ten times as busy for caterers. There are parties every day. For about five or six years in a row, I worked for Serves You Right Caterers at the house of the University of Southern California's president in Pasadena for the holidays. We did a Thanksgiving meal for many students who were not able to go home. And we then also did about nine sit-down dinners for various groups, organizations, and teachers at the school. Each night would be the same drill for a different group of guests.

One year, near that time, an event got pushed back to a later date due to a storm with 90 mile per hour wind gusts that blew over half the trees in the area and knocked out power. On our way to one of the Christmas events there, we saw many houses that had cut up wood left by the road from the downed trees. So, we picked some up, tossed it in our car trunk, and had plenty of firewood throughout that winter. In California, one might need it for only three nights during winter. It does go down to about 30 degrees once in a while in southern California. Many people don't know that.

Anyway, for these Christmas events we did, we were like robots. We would do the same exact thing for nine days in a row with maybe one day off in between. It was like being in the movie *Ground Hog's Day*. SAME exact Christmas music each day. The first night it was kind of nice to hear the Michael Bublé Christmas CD. I like him and his singing, but by the ninth day in a row hearing that CD, I wanted to bash his skull in.

To serve the dinners, we would line up in the kitchen. There would be four lines of chefs plating up the food, and the expediter would direct you to a line. He would point and say, "You go to number one, then point to the next servers and say, "You go to number two," "You go to number three," and so forth. One time, I was getting to the front of the line, and as he was directing people, he said to the person in front of me, "Go to line three," and then he turned to me and said, "Hold the line," and without missing a beat, I said, "Toto."

It took him a second, and then he laughed. "Hold the Line" is a song by the group Toto and he got the joke. One has to keep oneself amused to get through these events.

FIFTEEN

TALENTED PEOPLE I'VE CATERED WITH

At catering jobs, I was known not only for my singing (and I use that word *singing* loosely) while I work, but also for saying under my breath (and sometimes out loud), "My talents are being wasted," and, "Thank God my writing and producing career is taking off soon." The universe apparently must have thought I was being sarcastic. I said this for several years.

Hey, you do what you gotta do. And the truth is, very few reach the kind of success in the entertainment field to where they get paid enough to perform their art full time. To survive, the majority of performers do something on the side.

I think too many people end up just doing catering and leaving their dreams behind. Perhaps this book can inspire some (perhaps you?) to give up their survival jobs and put 100 percent into acting, singing, or making art, or to give them ideas on how to balance those jobs but still leave enough time to put into their passion.

Everyone has to do what is right and works best for them. The goal of many waiters and bartenders is to act or write, and only that, in order to support themselves and lead a decent life. Contrary to popular belief, not everyone doing acting wants to be a household name.

I actually am a household name. Everyone in my household knows my name LOL.

Sometimes the really hellish catering jobs I've done would inspire me to do my creative stuff more. I'd work hard for eight or ten hours for someone else and then think to myself, 'I should work as hard for myself and my projects as I do for a company that treats their employees poorly. It would inspire me to redouble my creative efforts.

Honest work is nothing to be ashamed of. So, kudos to those who do any side job, including catering, while pursuing their dreams and creative aspirations. My coworker and friend Gretchen Krull always joked with me at catering jobs, saying, "I don't want to see you," meaning "on catering jobs," because she thought my writing and acting work was good and that's what I should be doing all the time.

I worked with many talented people in catering. While many said they were actors, some were not going on auditions, taking classes, getting updated headshots, and such. It's relatively easy to get so sucked into catering that your goals get pushed to the back burner. (Yes, another catering pun for those keeping track!) Then all your time and energy is consumed by catering. One of my coworkers,

Christopher Ross Nygaard, who gave up catering quite a while back, puts it this way, "Catering is quicksand."

Then there are those who do catering who actually had the occasional success, or even a lot of it, and I would like to praise those people here, all of whom I had the pleasure of working with at some time. I love it when success at any level comes to good people I know.

The Marvelous Matilda Szydagis

I will start with Matilda Szydagis because she plays Zelda on one of my favorite shows, the multiple award-winning *Marvelous Mrs. Maisel*. I worked with Matilda while catering in New York many years ago. We connected on Facebook and stayed in touch. I was so happy to see her on a show which has won sixteen Emmys.

The role of Zelda is a great one in which Matilda is very funny. She's in several episodes. It was great to see her on stage with the cast, as they accepted their Screen Actors Guild Award.

I asked Matilda some questions.

What advice would you give to someone who wants to get into catering?

I would tell actors/creatives that catering is a great way to make money and have flexibility, although very tiring and physically draining. It certainly is a hustle. But you do make some really good friends while catering, especially if you stick to one or two companies and crew.

To all the ladies: LEARN TO BARTEND and work with catering companies who use lady bartenders. I was the only female bartender for YEARS at so many functions. Sadly, at least back in the day, many companies refused to use women as bartenders. I can only assume and hope that has changed now.

Tell me about some of your past creative projects and some upcoming ones.

I was getting ready for Season 4 of *The Marvelous Mrs. Maisel,* but COVID put a pause on that for the time being. It's been beyond an incredible experience being on the show and working with such amazing people, cast and crew alike. I'm super grateful!

I created three short horror films over the past few years that have been in the film fest circuit and are now on Amazon Prime. The films are called *The Hoosac, The Ruins,* and *The Dam*. My goal is to get them turned into features. I also just finished my book on my family's experiences during World War II and their subsequent immigration to North America. I was also in the middle of rehearsals directing a play when COVID came along.

Levi Kreis

Many years ago, I worked with a guy named Levi Kreis a few times in California. I remember him saying to me, "I'm a singer, I'm just doing this for a very short time." I only did see him a few times at catering jobs. I ran into him somewhere a couple years later, and he was doing well and has had many successes since then. He's won a Tony Award for "Best Featured Actor in a Musical," playing Jerry Lee Lewis in *Million Dollar Quartet.* Levi's other acting credits include Broadway's Tony-nominated revival of *Violet*, the national tour of *Rent, Smokey Joe's café,* and *Pump Boys and Dinettes*. Levi also does a great job in the movie, *A Very Sordid Wedding*, the sequel to *Sordid Lives*, both written and directed by Del Shores. He's put out several CDs, including *Imagine Paradise, Liberated,* and an EP called *Bad Habit.* Levi's music has been featured in film and television shows, including *The Vampire Diaries, Sons of Anarchy,* and *So You Think You Can Dance.*

It stuck with me just how determined Levi was. Those who really focus on their goals and have confidence are much more apt to make it. I'm so happy for him. He's a Facebook friend, and I love keeping up with all his accomplishments. He's an example of really going after your dream and knowing what you want.

Rick Negron

Rick Negron was one of the best captains for one of the worst caterers I ever worked for. Really nice guy. He had been in *Mamma Mia* in Las Vegas, on Broadway in *Man of La Mancha*, and *Kiss of the Spiderwoman* and *Leader of the Pack*. When he wasn't in a show, he did catering, as many do. He spent all of 2019 playing King George III in *Hamilton* in San Francisco and was supposed to continue all through 2020—then the coronavirus hit.

Some captains and butlers are bitter when they do catering—angry they are not doing what they want—but not

Rick. He was always pleasant, knew what he was doing, and treated everyone well.

I gave Rick a questionnaire.

What was one of the worst catering experiences you ever had?

There have been so many nightmare experiences. The Olesons definitely are in the top five. I also worked for REDACTED at the Ryder Cup, a golf event in Boston. I had a small satellite kitchen and one chef job catering for eight tents of 200-plus guests each for breakfast, lunch, and dinner. I would arrive at work at 5AM to start making coffee, hours before guest arrival, working with one coffee urn for eight tents.

At that job, I was so stressed that I lost my voice and ended up having vocal surgery later that year. However, the single worst experience for me was only a few years ago working for Wendy C. at Annapurna Films. It was a small cocktail party with dropped off hors d’oeuvres. Super easy party and an amazing group of captains working as butlers: Greg Phelan, Stephen Gatta, and Mark Smith. There were some big Hollywood players at the event, and Wendy was a raging bitch the entire evening. She was making nasty comments all night, while we were busting our asses and doing an amazing job for her.

At the end of the evening, she asked us to pack up all her decor items. Candles and decorations had to be boxed and carried out to her car. She kept yelling at us to go faster. When we were done, I lost my cool and turned around to her and said, “Between the four of us, there are close to eighty years of catering experience. We have all busted our butts working for you tonight, and there has not been a kind or gracious word from you: only criticism and nasty comments. I never want to work for you again. You are a miserable person, and you don't appreciate good people when they are doing their best."

She started weeping at the end of my tirade, and I said, "Save your crocodile tears for someone who gives a damn," and walked away.

Best one?

I spent an entire day at Jennifer Garner and Ben Affleck's home while they entertained the President of Rwanda. (Ben was involved with an NGO that works in the region.) I was working with one of my favorite chefs, Matt Poley, from Heirloom Catering, and we just had a wonderful stress-free day. Jennifer couldn't have been sweeter. I got to interact and play with their kids. Ben was his usual aloof self, but Jennifer gave me a $300 tip at the end of the day.

Tell us a little about your experience performing in *Hamilton* and other shows, or creative projects you've worked on.

My mom was the drama teacher in middle school, and I got the bug at an early age. I did my first professional musical at age ten. I danced on TV and in nightclubs in San Juan when I was fifteen. After college, I moved to New York and started working as a "triple threat" gypsy in 1985. I was in the chorus of five Broadway shows and three national tours and danced in Michael Jackson's "Bad" video. I played a reporter and danced in *Chicago*, the movie. Also played Sam in *Mamma*

Mia! in Vegas and then went on to play Kevin Rosario in the Broadway company of *In the Heights*.

Joining the And Peggy Tour cast of *Hamilton* has been a real dream come true. This company was assembled to join Lin Manuel Miranda in the one-month run of *Hamilton* in San Juan. We raised over 13 million dollars for arts education on the island, and for me, it was a homecoming like no other. I had tons of press and even was interviewed by *The New Yorker* magazine. Not to mention I have a New Yorker caricature now.

What advice would you give for anyone getting into catering?

It's a tough business, but we all do it for flexibility. It can be a trap. You sometimes get so busy with it that you lose your focus and stop prioritizing what really matters to you. However, I have made some wonderful friends and had some amazing experiences over the years. As a captain, I have always led by example. I treat people with kindness and respect. I try to inspire with humor and intellect. My mantra is: How you do one thing is how you do everything.

Biggest pet peeves from among the annoying things guests at an event do?

I hate people who are not gracious. It doesn't take much effort to acknowledge other people and appreciate their hard work.

Kevin Scott Allen

Kevin was one of my captains. One of those who does quite a bit of acting work between catering, including guest starring on *Prison Break* and *Alias*, and many other shows. He's also an acting teacher. I read and recommend his book called: *Conquering the Film and Television Audition.* He was in the original version of Terry Ray's play *Electricity,* and his performance was very powerful. The play later costarred Mel England. Both actors were very good in the play, as was the writer Terry Ray. It's very moving and ran several years in Palm Springs after being in Los Angeles.

Kevin also had the displeasure of working for "Mrs. Oleson." That vile woman will go down in catering history.

What was one of the worst catering experiences you ever had?

Standing in Mrs. Oleson's kitchen after a sit-down dinner, she asked me why fish forks weren't set on the table. I told her that we would set out all silverware we were to use per her houseman's specific instructions, so we set the table with what was put out. We weren't allowed to go into her silverware drawer. She then turned to her houseman in front of my entire staff and me, and screamed at him, calling him a liar, incompetent, and an idiot who didn't know a fish fork from a salad fork.

Best one?

After a sit-down dinner at Blythe Danner's house, as we broke down the dining room, in the next room Cheryl Crow and Melissa Etheridge sat at the piano and sang duets.

Tell us a little about your experience performing in TV shows and or creative projects you've worked on and about teaching acting.

I began acting on television when I was a kid, my first series a short-lived western, *Bearcats*. I had a recurring character on *The Waltons*, went to college, then I got back into acting. My best gig was as a regular on *Homefront*. Still, a pretty good second was getting to sing and dance with Ella Fitzgerald in a Disney special. She was so sweet to me, a dumb kid who didn't know who she was.

What advice would you give for anyone getting into catering?

Don't take anything personally. Clients, managers—all have their peculiarities, so just listen and adapt as best as possible. We know it's just a party, but for some folks, it's the second coming. Do your job, go home, and spend your check any way you want.

Biggest pet peeves from among annoying things guests at an event do?

Using fingers to pick up food off a buffet.

What projects or events do you have coming up that you are excited about?

I am working on an historical project, hopefully, for A&E and writing a book, a mystery set in Los Angeles.

Doug Campbell

Doug's a very nice guy whom I worked with when I first got to California. We catered together for Tommy Tang's catering.

We had a few things in common. We were both writers and Eddie Rabbit fans. I don't remember how we discovered that but I talk about music a lot, and I am a big country music fan, so it was bound to come up. Maybe it was raining at a catering event and I, being the singing waiter, started singing "I Love A Rainy Night," but who knows?

For the past twenty-plus years, Doug's been teaching acting and directing many Lifetime movies. Some of the films he directed for Lifetime were *Deadly Mile High Club, Stalked by My Mother*, and *Stalked by My Doctor* (starring Eric Roberts). He also wrote and directed *Marriage Killer* and *Dream Killer.*

These were his answers to my questionnaire.

What was one of the worst catering experiences you ever had?

I believe the last catering experience I had was my worst. It was at some hotel on Sunset Boulevard, and we ran out of food. They asked me to wait on people like a restaurant waiter, and I suck at that because I have no short-term memory. The guests had to park across the street for $40 for three hours, which pissed off the guests. There was practically a mutiny from the guests altogether—a bloody disaster.

The second-worst catering experience was when this company tried to stiff me for 125 bucks. I took them to court and got the jerkwad to pay. I should have pushed my luck and had him pay me for the days he was late—which would have pushed my paycheck north of three grand. Instead, the guy reached into his pocket, took out $125 cash, and handed it to me. I told him he was a jerk for treating people that way. That was it.

Best one?

High school, working for a wonderful lady and friend who ran her own sub shop and catering business at age twenty-four. She was generous, fun, and fair. Just great.

Tell us a little about your experience as a director or creative projects you've worked on, and about teaching acting.

I've been writing and directing feature films and television professionally since 1987, with some down years. Because of runaway production in the late 1990s, I was out of work entirely. My girlfriend, who was doing some catering, got me back into it, just as a hired hand—never a cook or running a catering business. Lately, I've been writing and directing features that air on LMN and Lifetime. In May of 2020, a film I directed premiered called *Deadly Mile High Club.* When we do *Deadly Caterer,* I suppose I'll need to hire Rick Karatas to write it!

Speaking of Rick (Sudi), I remember passing hors d'oeuvres at a party with the incredible Rick Karatas. I was moving through the guests, and I recognized a pretty face. She recognized me. She smiled, and so did I. "Doug? Hi!" she said.

"Hi, Joanna," I said. "Hungry?" I offered her some filo stuffed with spinach.

I'm not kidding. She had just auditioned for me for a movie I directed a few months earlier. But because I had worked so long on the film (writing, developing, and doing post-production), I was out of bucks and needed to earn some money to pay rent. (I didn't cast her, but she was a very talented actress.) So, there I was, back on the catering job with probably thirteen years of professional experience directing films and television behind me—doing whatever it takes to stay ahead of the taxman.

These days when I'm directing, I make sure to go through the chow line last (so no crewmember or actor goes hungry, in case they run out), and I have a special place in my heart for the people who cater our films. I tell them that I used to cater a lot, and we talk about the trade.

What advice would you give for anyone getting into catering?

Get paid the night you cater, at the end of the job, if you can. Make that a requirement right at the top. If your boss balks, he may stiff you later on. There was a lot of exploitation going on back in the 1990s that I heard because bosses were taking advantage of actors and movie hopefuls just arriving in L.A.. Sadly, I've found that you gotta hound these people (not all—some). One gig, they were seven weeks late paying. I called the catering company around week six and said, "Hey, Marty, are you guys alright?"

Marty said, "Yeah, we're fine."

I said, "Everything's okay, really? You're not sick?"

Marty said, "No, I feel great."

"How about your partner? He okay?"

"He's fine!"

"Everything okay with the business? I mean, are you guys in good shape?"

He said with a laugh, "We're fine!"

"You're not filing for bankruptcy or anything?" I said.

"NO!" he bellowed, laughing. "Not at all. We're doing great! Jesus!"

And then I said, "Okay, then tell me why you can't pay me the money you owe me for a catering job I did for you six weeks ago?"

Oh, you should have heard him stammer and ya-dee-yadda, trying to bullshit his way out of that one. Finally, they paid. But you gotta hound 'em.

Biggest pet peeves from among the annoying things guests at an event do?

One guest tried to basically invite my girlfriend (another girlfriend from back in the 1980s) to sleep with him. So, I put some barbecue sauce on the back of my hand and "accidentally" smeared it on the back of his white, camel hair sport coat.

True story.

Don't tell anybody.

What projects or events do you have coming up that you are excited about?

I have a couple projects coming up! Twenty-twenty was going to be a banner year for me. Now? Thanks to COVID-19, dead in the water. So, I'm writing. I've got about twenty or so films airing on LMN on a rotating basis. I'm very lucky.

Keir Kirkegaard

Keir is an actor, singer, dancer, and all-around nice guy. He performed in *Rock of Ages* in Vegas and *Mamma Mia* at the Hollywood Bowl, and in the musical *Edward Scissorhands.* He was also on a *Tosh.0* episode on Comedy Central with his lovely wife Andi (Davis) Kirkegaard, an actress and singer. She makes the best cookies at her own company Kirki Kookies by Andi.

This is the questionnaire Keir filled out.

What was one of the worst catering experiences you ever had?

I was working for a very famous music producer at his house in the Hidden Hills. I have worked for him several times and each time seemed to get more and more ridiculous. This particular party was just him and his family, about six people. There were three of us on staff to do bar and very detailed service. He flew a chef in from Atlanta, and among the many things that she made was fried chicken. The kitchen did not have a fryer, so she fried it on the stovetop, but did all of the prep work on the kitchen island. She took the breaded chicken from the island and walked it across to the stove, making a huge mess along the way.

As she was cooking, the three of us working kept looking in the kitchen and shaking our heads, knowing that it was going to be a big clean up job for us. The party went by, the service was fine, and when we finally got into the kitchen to start the cleanup, it was around midnight. We had been there since 4 PM, so it was already a long shift, and the kitchen was a nightmare. Grease and oil were everywhere! And when I say *everywhere,* I mean, literally everywhere: the floor, the island, the stovetop, all around both sinks, in every hard to reach clean spot imaginable. What made it really bad was the chef and the host sat in the kitchen for the first hour pointing out all the spots that we were missing and telling us to make sure to get it all cleaned up.

By the time it hit 4 AM, I had to stop checking my phone because I was getting so angry that we were still there cleaning, and so mad that the chef made such a mess for no reason. We ended up leaving at 6:30 AM, making it a fourteen-and-a-half-hour shift and the worst shift I ever had. To top it all off, we did not get paid for that shift for nine months, and the only reason we finally did was that we hired a lawyer and threatened to sue.

Best one?

I certainly have more stories of great shifts than horror stories. For the most part, the business has been wonderful, and 99 percent of the people I have worked for have been incredibly nice and caring. I have two that are tied for the lead as my best shifts.

When I first got into the business, I worked a lot of celebrity parties in Hollywood. Awards season was always the time to work parties that were loaded with A-listers. At one of them, I was walking around bussing tables. I approached one with a very famous actress. As I walked up to clean the table, she stopped her conversation, looked at me as if I was interrupting the most important conversation ever, did not say a word, or help me grab all of the plates. As I left, I heard her huff and say, "Wow . . . well, anyway . . ." Needless to say, I was not in a great mood, but I was also now gun shy about going up to tables. I saw that Channing Tatum was sitting at a table by himself and had plates all over it. I walked up as politely as I could and started to clean, making sure not to disturb him. He stopped eating his food, started to help me stack all of the plates, looked me in the eyes, and said, "Thank you so much!"

He entirely made my night, and it was a great learning lesson for me to never forget the importance of being kind to others.

The other one was actually not a very fun place to work. The house and service were very formal, and I was always the extra server working with people that worked there a lot—meaning, I always got assigned the bad jobs. However, one night, out of eight guests, one of them was Sidney Poitier. I am too young to have seen him in his prime, but I was familiar with him and his work. When I first greeted him at the door, he actually took the time to look me in the eye, ask me for my name, use my name back, and say thank you. This may seem like common human decency, but in the world of catering, so many times, we are completely invisible and just there to do a job. So, for him to stop and take the time to do that was very nice.

Later, during a cocktail hour, I brought him a drink, and he stopped the conversation, made up a poem on the spot using my name, and again said, "Thank you." Upon leaving, he shook my hand, used my name again, and said goodnight. He is the definition of a gentleman, and eight years later, I can still remember what an impression that made on me.

Tell us a little about your experience performing in shows like *Edward Scissorhands* and other shows in Vegas or creative projects you've worked on.

I have had some wonderful experiences on stage. I toured with a musical through Asia and Australia for a year, worked on cruise ships, in Las Vegas on *Rock of Ages,* got to be in *Mamma Mia* at the Hollywood Bowl, and performed in lots of local theater in L.A. and Colorado. *Rock of Ages* in Las Vegas has to be at the top for me. It was one of the first Broadway shows I had ever seen, and I saw it on my trip to New York as a senior in college.

We got the last tickets they had left, and they were standing room only in the back of the mezzanine. Still, to this day, it is the most fun I have ever had in a theater seeing a show, and I remember specifically saying to myself, *I am going to be in this show one day.*

At the time, I really wanted to play the character Franz. When they sang "Every Rose Has Its Thorn," I got lost in the thought of being in the show. Fast forward five years, and I booked the male swing role in Vegas, playing six parts, one of them being Franz. One of my first nights going on, we got to the point in the show where we sing "Every Rose Has It's Thorn," and I was so happy and content. I had wanted this for so long and finally had my chance to be on that stage at that moment.

During this part of the show, the audience pulls out fake lighters or cellphones and waves them back and forth. It is really magical to watch from the stage. About halfway through the song, I feel a push on my shoulder. It was the actress playing Regina, and she pushed me because it was my solo, and I wasn't singing. I abruptly came in halfway through the line, but it was apparent that I missed the first part.

After the show, she asked me what happened. I sheepishly said, "I was sitting there thinking about how amazing it is to be doing this show and how happy I am to be here singing this line in the show." Needless to say, I never missed that line again.

What advice would you give for anyone getting into catering?

Take pride in every event that you work. Sometimes the job can be rough and really draining on the soul, but always take pride in what you do. It is your job to create a wonderful experience for the guest, whether they are an A-list celebrity or someone you have never heard of.

Biggest pet peeves from among annoying things guests at an event do?

When you are trying to serve hors d'oeuvres or drinks, guests don't even look at you. They just use hand gestures to shoo you away. I have gotten to the point where I politely force them to look at me and be decent human beings.

Marc Copage

I really get to work with some wonderful people, like Marc Copage. He was a child star on the groundbreaking show *Julia,* which was the first television sitcom to star an independent and non-stereotypical African American woman in the title role. He played her son, Morey, on the show. He mostly bartended the events I did. Always a pleasure to work with. He returned to school to study jazz improvisation. I'm proud to call him a friend. He has an autobiography coming out, *Television's First Black Child Star*.

"Excuse Me, Waiter, I Speak Jive"

I was working an event around, maybe, 2010? And I was having a conversation with one of the other waiters, whom I had not worked with before. Come to find out he was in the movie *Airplane,* which is one of my all-time favorite movies. He told me he was one of the two black guys speaking jive with the main character, played by Julie Haggarty, and Barbara Billingsley from the TV show *Leave It to Beaver*. He had only a few lines, but EVERYONE knows that scene. The waiter/actor was very nice. He said that twenty-five years after the film came out, he still gets invited to conventions for the movie where people still ask for his autograph.

I was sad to think that he had this part in a classic movie that everyone knew, and years later, he is doing catering. But he actually seemed to enjoy it and be happy, and that's really all that matters. After that, I never saw him, so maybe he's getting a lot of acting work, or perhaps he became a pilot or is teaching jive in a school somewhere?

A Few More Talented People I've Worked With

I want to mention a few more talented people I've worked with over the years like:

- David A. Lee and Daniel Vaillancourt: Two nice, talented guys who are also a married couple. They were the writers for the MTV show *Undressed* and the 19th

Annual GLAAD Media Awards in 2008. David is also a gifted photographer, David A. Lee Photography in Palm Springs. Daniel does some acting as well. They wrote the short film *Like Father* in 2017, directed by Jason Stuart, who acted in my film, *Walk a Mile in My Pradas.*

- John Riccio: A singer/songwriter, one of his compositions was featured in my film *Walk a Mile in My Pradas*, an instrumental. He has a beautiful CD, *Tomorrow Is What It Used To Be,* with songs he wrote. I made him mad once at an event. He was carrying a heavy dish of something and looking for one of the buffets. He asked me, "Where is buffet three?" and I, being the wiseass I am, said, "Two lights, then make a right to the third stop sign," as the platter was getting heavier and heavier in his hand. He yelled at me, "Can you ever just answer a question seriously?" We laugh about it now. At least I do. But seriously, he is a great singer and songwriter.
- Joseph F. Alexandre: Directed the award-winning documentary, *Warriors of the Discotheque: The Starck Club Documentary* and the documentary *The Real Casino*.
- Marie Todd: A stand-in for Melissa Leo in *I'm Dying Up Here*, she was in my movie *Walk a Mile in My Pradas*, many of my sketches on YouTube, and in my Christmas music videos *All I Want for Christmas Is Some Sleep* and *Midnight Will Be Clear*. She danced in the Grammy Award-winning video *Old Town Road* by Billy Ray Cyrus and Lil Nas. (A few million more people saw that video than my Christmas videos).

- Robert Catrini: Worked as a captain. He had a big part in the film *Jack Reacher,* doing a couple scenes with Tom Cruise and had big roles in *Birds of Prey* and *G.I. Joe,* and he's done around one hundred costar and guest star roles.
- Michael McCaul: Everyone calls him "Moneyball" because he was a stand-in for Brad Pitt in the movie of the same name. He's also done work in several other movies.
- Joey Thomas: A captain who did staffing for one of the companies I worked for. She performed a double role in the play *Gideon's Knot*—alternating each night. I worked with her on a commercial written by Andrew Ortiz for the company Kelly's Cleaning in Reading, Pennsylvania.
- Frank Perry: Also acted in my film and some of my sketches on YouTube. He was excellent in the play *The Deadly Game* in a theater in Long Beach, California. He was the lead in the film *Expose* by Ronja Janz, a comedy short and won many awards in Europe. He also made another film with her, a longish short called *Annabel Lee*.
- Jeff Karr: He has a funny line in my movie, *Walk a Mile in My Pradas,* and does stunt work.
- Kristy Munden: Guest starred on *West World.* She was one of the few on there who got to keep their clothes on. She's also been on *Jimmy Kimmel Live* and *Grey's Anatomy.*
- Michael Albala: Good captain, also a good actor.

- Eric Yoste: Is a talented writer.
- Joey Sylvester: Directed my movie, *Walk a Mile in My Pradas,* and the film *Amanda and The Fox.*
- Karla Guy: Is in many of my YouTube sketches, including *The Phone Sex Operator,* which got about 200,000 views. She has also edited many of my sketches.

There are many more, but these are the ones that popped in my head. Those I forgot, I will mention when I accept my Oscar. I wish all those I've catered with success in all their future creative endeavors.

SIXTEEN

IN MEMORIAM

THOSE NO LONGER WITH US

I joke that catering sucked the life right out of me, but I think there is something about it shortening our lifespans. Quite a few people I've catered with seem to have left us way too soon, so I want to acknowledge them and let the world know they made a difference. These coworkers, who are no longer with us, were not known to the whole world, but they were known to the catering world and to their friends and families and I am honored to include them here.

Chef Matt Bencivenga

Chef Matt Bencivenga was one of the kindest men I ever knew in the food industry. He always made sure we got something to eat and he was always laid back and friendly. He bravely fought pancreatic cancer for seven years while still working as a chef and keeping up his good attitude. About a month before he died, I worked an event at the Rose Bowl. It was very early in the morning and we were both trying to find exactly where we had to go. It was a little confusing, and I was a little flustered. He was calm and said, "At least we're here." Despite everything, he was in good spirits and happy to be there. I didn't know that a month or so later he would be gone.

My friend Marie remembers having nice conversations with Matt about horseracing, a passion they both shared. A 1,500-person event could be going on, but he would find a few minutes to chat with her about horseracing topics, such as who was running that day.

Several years before he passed, long before he was sick, I was having a small fundraising party to get some funds to shoot my film *Walk a Mile in My Pradas*. I mentioned it to him and asked if he could possibly donate one appetizer or something for it. He said, "Sure stop by the kitchen the day of the event." I did and he had a whole bunch of stuff for me. Shrimp with cocktail sauce, tea sandwiches, chocolate chip cookies, and a couple other things. It was just so nice of him to do that. I really would have been happy with just one item. He died very young—I believe in his early forties. I will always remember his generosity and kindness.

Valerie Moore

If I am the "king of puns," Valerie Moore, whom I worked with for many years, was the "queen of puns." She once went to a party where the theme was to dress up in a "period piece." She came as a tampon. Another costume she did once was "Waste of Time," in which she had little boxes of the condiment thyme all around her waist.

Valerie provided much-needed comic relief during catering events. For instance, she would be carrying a plate of fish to a table while singing, "Salmon chanted evening" (sung to the melody of "Some Enchanted Evening"). I always enjoyed working with her because we shared the same sense of humor. Once she was holding a bread roll in her hand and striking all sorts of poses and she asked, "What am I?" I had no idea. She said with a straight face, "A role model."

She also taught me what "crop dusting" is. If it were getting late and some guests just would not leave, she would say, "It's time to do some crop dusting."

I said, "What's that?" and she told me. You walk around the guests letting out silent but deadly farts, so they will leave. Sometimes they just stand there making faces, wondering which one cut the cheese while the perpetrator is long gone.

I enjoyed working with her and was saddened to hear when she passed away too young, I think in her forties. Amy Lieberman Judd with whom I've worked remembers Valerie as "one of the most intelligent, unique people I have ever met, and she always made working a catering event more interesting. When I showed up at a shift and Val was there, I knew I'd at least have a few laughs."

Eva

I don't remember her last name, but when I used to work with Fran Zaslow Caterers (when Fran was the owner) about twenty-five years ago, there was a lovely woman named Eva, who was one of the cooks. I just remember she was always so pleasant and had such a good attitude. She was a little bit heavy, then she got cancer and I watched her become smaller. She passed away shortly after that. I really only worked with her a short period, but I remember her all these years later as a sweet and kind woman.

Here's what Fran had to say about her. "One of my best supervisors and right-hand cooks was the beloved Eva. She was the smartest worker ever! Way smarter than me. But she always deferred to my cooking. She died of the same cancer Jaqueline Kennedy Onassis succumbed to."

Maggy (Margaret Ann) Holmes

Maggy was a very sweet woman from Ireland whose life was ended by cancer. The last time I saw her was at an Oscar event in 2017. My job for the Oscars that year was to hand out parking passes to the employees working the event.

I knew Maggy was very sick. She looked very thin and frail. I gave her a gentle hug and told her it was so good to see her. We hadn't seen her for a long time because she hadn't been working due to her illness. She was heading back to Ireland that week to spend her last days there, but she wanted to say goodbye to everyone she worked with. In some ways, the people who cater together really were a family—maybe a dysfunctional one, but a family.

I found out recently from Marie Todd that Maggy had a previous career working in fashion design. She attended FIDM in downtown L.A., short for the Fashion Institute of Design and

Merchandising. Our coworkers had so many talents and interests beyond catering that sometimes went unnoticed.

She passed away in Ireland a couple months after our last meeting. I will miss her and her sweet Irish accent.

My coworker and friend Tia Roberts was close to Maggy and here are her thoughts on her: "My dear friend Maggy Holmes was the second friend I made in catering. She was the hardest working person there and the consummate professional. Maggy loved working events and meeting people. She loved keeping souvenirs and if she weren't working a specific event that I was, she'd always ask me to grab one, which I happily would.

"She had a fantastic sense of humor and was the most loyal friend one can ask for. We were the truest of friends. She was encouraging, trustworthy, loving, forgiving, and the first one to offer help. We were each other's 'it' person. Whether dropping/picking each other up at the airport/fly away or I-need-your-help" situations, we were there for one another—we were family. We held hands and hugged each other through loss and hard times, and we laughed and celebrated all the great moments in between. She is in my heart forever and I miss her daily."

Krysta Florczyk remembers: "Maggy popped in to work the Oscars one last time and said, 'I love you,' and gave a big hug and I realized, *I'm never going to see her again.* To be so emotional at the Oscars over something that has nothing to do with the Oscars! Maggy made everything better. I was always glad to see that she was on a shift with me, and I would say to myself, *Thank God, Maggy's here."*

Keith Johnson, one of the very nice chefs I've worked with, remembers Maggy as a beautiful soul, who had a heart of gold. He said, "I loved saying hello to her and hearing her beautiful Irish accent. She was always so pleasant and had great sense of humor with true sincerity. I will miss her always."

Will Mathieu

I didn't know him that well, worked with him several times over several years. We don't always work with the same people, as there are many events and there are so many of us. But he seemed nice and I would talk to him a little, once in a while. He actually worked the event with me that I walked off of because of an arrogant obnoxious captain, and he confirmed to me that said captain, Anthony at Pocomotion events, was drunk, which I had told their owner.

Tragically, Will ended up jumping off a roof and killing himself. I think he was about forty. So young. Someone told me about an event he was at, and I'm not sure how close it was to when he ended his life, but there was a guest (the wealthy owner of famous buildings in L.A. who owned more houses than people have trashcans) and he saw that the bartender wasn't smiling. It was Will. The wealthy guest told the captain or supervisor of the event to send him home because he wasn't smiling. What a prick.

He had no idea what might be going on in the bartender's life. Will wasn't being rude or not doing his job, he just wasn't smiling enough for this rich a-hole.

You never know what's going on with someone in their lives or when someone might need help. It doesn't help the situation by sending them home from a job just because of some wealthy a-hole, who doesn't even tip people, according to those who worked in his house. Shame on the caterer for appeasing this kind of hateful person.

Quote from Rick Negron: "Will and I worked together many times. He was always kind, sweet, and funny. That can make a big difference when you're working a long shift at a stressful event."

Chef Vaughn

Chef Vaughn had long dreadlocks, usually kept under a Rasta hat. He was always pleasant, in a good, very chill, and laidback mood. I worked many events with him over the years. He never seemed to be in a bad mood. I was shocked when he died of an accidental overdose of some tainted drug. He was only about fifty. The caterer did a very nice memorial service for him. Many people spoke about how he had touched their lives.

Chef Marcos Rodriguez had this to say about him. "I owe my career to Chef Vaughn. I owe him for confidence, and I owe him for opening the many doors he did for me to walk through. He took to me and would always let me know what I did very well to help build me up. Chef was a man unto himself and the things I admired about him was his creating his career that started out at dishwashing. I admired his inherent ability for great food, structure and his generous heart to help others reach their potential."

John Hildendorf

Krysta called him "Sunshine," a little sarcastically, as he didn't exactly have a good positive outlook. He complained a lot and didn't really want to work but was not a bad guy. I think he wins the prize for taking the most cigarette breaks. Krysta told me that he would take a couple plates to someone, then ask if she put it in the captain report. His knee hurt often so he had to sit down a lot. Krysta said, "In the end, I even liked seeing Sunshine—at least I knew what to expect."

Once I was at an urgent care center. I don't even remember what my issue was, but I was waiting on my little cot in the area where they put those white curtains around you and you're in that night gown that reveals your butt, and I had to go to the bathroom. So, I was walking toward the restroom when, in another one of the little curtain areas, who did I see? John Hildendorf! He needed to have his gallbladder taken out.

My friend Frank Perry who worked with both John and me, remembers that once he was driving on the freeway to an event on the USC campus and this big guy on a tiny motorcycle pulled up next to him at the same speed really close to his window, and Frank wondered, "Why is this guy so close to my car? Frank realized it was John Hildendorf with a big shit-eating grin on his face just before John shot on ahead.

He died suddenly, not sure from what but we miss the big lug.

Steven Poole

Nice guy from the UK that I worked with in New York for a caterer there. He was only thirty-seven when he died from cancer. I remember he was a big Shania Twain fan. Always joking around with me. I went to visit him on his last birthday when he was in the hospital. He looked so thin. I was very saddened when he passed away. He kept up catering almost to the very end, which is hard enough to do when you're healthy and even harder when you're not.

My friend Francesca who worked with us remembers Steven fondly. When she was thinking of getting her naval pierced, he gently asked, "Are you sure?" She says: "I knew he was a truthteller and that my Buddha belly (at the time) wasn't the best canvas for the piercing. I never got it done and still remember that funny conversation. Love him."

Melissa DiNicola

Michele Gan, the owner of Serves You Right Caterers, for whom I enjoyed working, had a niece who worked with us a few times. I remember Melissa DiNicola as being very nice. I was shocked to hear that she had passed away in 2018 at only twenty-six years old from cancer. I didn't know at the time what a talented writer she was or that she was one of the writers on the show *Grace and Frankie* starring Lily Tomlin and Jane Fonda. Melissa cowrote the season four finale, and at the end of the episode bears a title card that reads: "This season is dedicated to the loving memory of Melissa DiNicola."

Per DiNicola's Instagram, she worked on the show for all five seasons, starting as a writer's assistant, and later moving into a position as a full-time staff writer on the show. So sad when someone dies that young, yet she accomplished more than many in a lifetime professionally. She wrote for an award-winning show.

Eileen Marie Smylie

Eileen was sweet and had a great sense of humor. We worked together about twenty-five years ago and reconnected on Facebook a few years before she passed from cancer. I think she was only in her forties—so sad. I remember one event where a guest was being rude and she leaned into the table, tugging on her ear, and said, "I didn't hear the P word."

Of course, Eileen meant the word *please.*

Many years later when I was in Palm Springs, I said that line, remembering her. "Excuse me, I didn't hear the P word," and being in Palm Springs, someone immediately said, "Penis?"

One of the good things about Facebook is finding friends from the past and being able to reconnect with them. I found this exchange from Facebook which took place a year before she died.

Eileen: When we'd be waiting around when we were at an event, I always got so happy when I saw you, we all had a laugh ☺))))

Me: Yes, then the event started, and we were miserable. lol

Eileen: Exactly!!!

Miss you, sweet Eileen.

Chef Mae Gabriel

Chef Mae was a very nice woman who worked for one of the same caterers as me. She was survived by a twelve-year-old child when she died. Very sad. The following was posted on Facebook in May 2020, when the protests were going on over the racial issues with police. Chef Mae was African American.

Richie Weber posted:

Today I am thinking about our great colleague Chef Mae. Several years back I was working with her at L.A. Live and she brought her father in to meet us. He shared with us that he marched with Dr. King in the Civil Rights movement. Looking at him, for me, he was as grand and eloquent as Dr. King himself. Mae is gone now, died far too soon of cancer, leaving behind a young son. I hope her son realizes what a great mother he had and a magnificent granddad. I will never forget that day.

A Few Others

I remember a nice guy named Jonah who was a houseman. In his twenties, he ended up getting shot. I think he was mistaken for a gang member. I remember another guy we worked with who died in a car accident. His brother worked with us too and he was only in his twenties. There was a woman named Margaret who killed herself. I didn't know her very well, but I remember how saddened I was by her death.

There are probably a few more I have worked with over the years that are no longer with us and if they are reading this from somewhere, thanks for being in my life, even if it was simply to clear a plate or two together.

SEVENTEEN

IDEAS WHILE CATERING

I get many ideas while catering because my mind wanders. At one event, the guests were eating like there was no tomorrow and, by the end of the shift, I had a whole chorus written for a song called "Let's Love Tonight Like There's No Tomorrow."

Once I got an idea for a full script at an event. It was a fundraiser where the hosts were auctioning off the most adorable puppy. I thought to myself, *What if that puppy is not supposed to be auctioned off? What if it's a mistake or an accident?* I had a logline by the time the event ended, and wrote a whole script called "The Auction" shortly thereafter.

Here are the logline and synopsis.

THE AUCTION

Logline: A little boy goes in search of his dog that was lost during a hurricane in New Orleans and is accidentally auctioned off to a rich, evil woman.

Synopsis: Little eight-year-old Danny is heartbroken when his family cannot find their dog "Mutt" as they evacuate due to an approaching hurricane in New Orleans. When they return home, there is no sign of his beloved pet and everyone assumes Mutt has gone to the "great big dog pound in the sky" —everyone except Danny who knows in his heart that his dog is alive. He happens to be right. The dog was found and then accidentally sold at an auction when it was thought his owners perished in the storm. Ms. Butterly, a wicked old woman who hates animals, accidentally bids on the dog as she shoos away a fly with her auction paddle. Ten thousand dollars later, she is the owner of the furry devil.

Ms. Butterly makes Luther, her butler/chauffer/ bodyguard and an aspiring musician, take care of Mutt until he had enough, quits, and leaves her with the dog. Several months later, Danny runs into Luther who recognizes the picture of Mutt that Danny shows him and tells him the dog is alive. Danny's parents don't believe him. They think he is in denial, so they take him to a psychiatrist. Then he runs away to find the dog.

In the meantime, Mutt saves his new owner's life from a thief who tries to rob her house. Ms. Butterly can't help but like the dog now and wants to keep him even after Danny shows up at her door to reclaim Mutt. She lies and says she doesn't have him. The boy finally rescues the dog and starts back home as another hurricane approaches putting him and Mutt in danger.

....

I hope this script will get made, but Hollywood only makes sequels and remakes so I will change the name to *The Auction 2.*

The Highly Allergic Customer

Before another event, the captains went over all the allergies of the guests that would be attending. The list was longer than a CVS cash register receipt with so many ridiculous things on it. I don't even remember what they were, but it gave me an idea for a sketch to take the absurdity even further. I later shot the sketch with Tom Archdeacon for my sketch comedy cable show *Skits and Giggles.* I'm guessing three people have seen it.

Waiter's Last Night Sketch

I wrote a funny sketch about a waiter where I played the waiter (a huge stretch for me) and my friends and fellow actors Marie Todd and Frank Perry played the couple. We had fun. You can check it out on YouTube. It got a little over 7,000 views, but once this book sells a million copies I expect that number to go up. It was directed by Mark Katz, a very nice and talented guy, who directed and helped with many of my sketches for my show *Skits and Giggles* on public access. Check out the sketch at https://youtu.be/dnjFDQih1ko.

This is the script to that sketch:

INT. RESTAURANT—NIGHT

Man and his wife sit at a table. The grumpy man is on his cellphone.

Man:

Good, go with that one.

He hangs up.

Man:

Why isn't our food here yet?

Woman:

At least we have the nice waiter this time.

The waiter brings the salads and puts them down.

Man:

Finally.

Waiter:

That's a great tie by the way.

Man:

Should be. It cost a grand.

Woman:

Does this have the fat-free dressing on it, like I asked for?

Waiter:

Yes, but believe me, you don't need to worry about fat-free dressing with that figure.

The man gives him a dirty look.
The waiter's cell phone rings in his pocket.

Man (*annoyed*):

Is that your phone?

Waiter:

Yeah sorry. Excuse me.

He turns his back to them and picks up.

Man:

What? It did? Oh My God, that's great.

The waiter turns around, demeanor totally changed.

Waiter:

You done with these?

Woman:

Yes, the lettuce was wilted though.

Man:

And my tomato was not ripe enough and would you bring me another drink, this drink is not strong enough

Waiter:

Okay. Scotch on the rocks, less rocks.

Woman:

And could you ask them to hurry? We're pressed for time.

Waiter:

Yes, I know. Every time you come in here you are pressed for time and every time his drink is not strong enough and *(voice rising)* every time there is a problem with the food!

The waiter storms off.

Woman:

What's come over him?

Man:

I don't know but I don't like his attitude.

The waiter returns with the plate and takes a huge sip out of the guy's glass.

Waiter:

Yup! Definitely strong enough.

Man:

You drank out of my drink.

Waiter:
Quality control.

Man:
I cannot drink this drink now, and this is definitely not what I ordered.

Waiter:
Yes, it is, but if you like I can have the kitchen make you something else, that you probably won't like, and that's gonna take a little time and you're in a hurry so why don't I just give you the check.

Man:
This is unacceptable, get me the manager.

Waiter:
I don't care. I don't need this crummy job anymore. I just got a call from NBC. The pilot I just wrote got picked up by them.

Man:
Congratulations.

Waiter:
Thank you.

Man:

What was your name again?

Waiter:

Anthony. Anthony Nucci. Remember it because you're going to be hearing it a lot in the future.

The man takes out his cell phone.

Man:

Yeah, change of plans. Instead of the Nucci pilot, let's go with that Bill guy's script.

The waiter looks at the guy, suddenly recognizing him.

Waiter:

Oh my god, you're the head of development at NBC! I knew I knew you from somewhere.

The couple gets up in disgust.

Waiter:

Oh wait, shoot, you've been punked. We've got Ashton Kutcher in the kitchen—

Man:

That show went off the air a long time ago.

The couple leaves.

Waiter:

I'm so fired.

EIGHTEEN

MISCELLANEOUS MISHAPS AND CATERING CHAOS

Many crazy things happen at events, some of which I've talked about but there are a few more I would like to share that myself and coworkers experienced.

Putting Out Fires, Literally

One time I was standing behind my buffet, which I will say was buffet four, because how would I remember years later what real number it was? Sometimes there were up to eighteen of them. Guests were coming through the line. I heard over my walkie talkie, "This is buffet five. I don't have a fire extinguisher at my buffet." I decided to look under my buffet to see if I had one. Sure enough, I didn't have one either. I called on the walkie and said, "This is buffet four, I don't have a fire extinguisher either." Then the other buffets proceed to do the same thing, each one announcing that they also didn't have a fire extinguisher under their buffet tables.

Later on, we found out that the first buffet that had called actually had a fire. A can of Sterno (fuel) had tipped over and lit the tablecloth on fire. I was shocked. The person behind the buffet had just calmly said they didn't have an extinguisher, not that their buffet was on fire! This is the kind of person I guess I want around in a crisis, someone who can remain that calm when their buffet is on fire!

Why Do I Smell Marshmallows?

I worked with Adam Butter, many years ago who has remained a good friend. We worked together with Corrine's Concepts, a nice caterer on Long Island who is still around. Adam has been doing real estate for many years on Long Island and is with Engel & Völkers in Long Beach.

One time, Adam and I were working a party in Brooklyn, New York, in an apartment for a private client. Something was in the oven that we had to take out. We were searching all over for an oven mitt or dish towel. We finally found one and, as I reached in to get the food item, I turned to say something to Adam, and suddenly he said, "Why do I smell marshmallows?"

And I'm like, "Yeah, I do too," which was weird because we were inside, and we weren't making s'mores or anything. I turned to look back in the oven and the dish towel I was holding must have touched the burner because it was on fire. That's what we were smelling.

I was freaking out, trying to put it out, and finally we threw it in the sink and turned the water on. I felt bad that we burned what looked like a brand-new dish towel. We hid it at the bottom of the garbage bag, made sure a lot of stuff was covering all the evidence, and out it went to the trash to be lost like a sock in the dryer.

Fire in Malibu

These next two stories were told to me by Jer Girma, one of my coworkers.

It was fire season in California, and there was a fire not too far from an event she was working that was burning out of control. Ashes were coming down on them as they worked outside on a big tennis court. People were wearing masks (this was years before coronavirus)—that's how bad the air was. It was raining ashes and the air was hard to breathe, so the staff had their masks and sunglasses on to keep their eyes from burning.

The host told the captain that the staff needed to take them off and the captain had a fight with her. She then requested that he leave, so before the event even started, he went home and all the butlers were told they couldn't wear them, although they could leave if they wanted.

At another outdoor event that Jer worked, they had no kitchen. There was a food truck and seating outside. One cook put the spray oil too close to the stove and it exploded, so they had to leave the area. Part of the truck was on fire and the fire department came.

Krysta Fire Story

Krysta Florczyk told me about an event where the DGA (Directors Guild of America) was almost set on fire. The tree caught on fire in the kitchen. There were flames shooting up trees, near propane tanks. Krysta thought to herself, *If this is the day, this is the day.*

She says, "I thought I might be a goner." After that event, she called her dad and said, "If I ever die in a catering event, I just want you to know I love you."

Hailstorm

Like the mailman, we work through all kinds of weather. I worked a party outside in a hailstorm in Los Angeles as the band continued to play, and guests were all given ponchos and huddled under umbrellas near heat lamps. It is very rare to have rain, let alone hail, in Los Angeles in the summer.

As you can see we've dealt with fire and ice on events.

Broken Toe at Tavern on the Green

I was supposed to break a leg acting. Instead, I broke a toe catering.

I was working at Tavern on the Green in Central Park in Manhattan, carrying a huge center piece, and the heavy bottom fell off and broke my toe. It happened after the event, as we were breaking everything down. It hurt like hell. I got home at about 3:00 AM, took some aspirin, and tried to sleep. The toenail turned black and blue and fell off a month later. That is the only body part I have ever broken, and other than my pride being hurt, it was the only thing I ever injured at an event. Most catering events I've done were usually safe.

Sex in the Pool

No, I did not have sex in the pool—at least not at a catering event I worked. We did some events by a pool at a hotel next to one of our venues in Hollywood. One morning around 5:30 AM, we were setting up tables and chairs and buffets. It was still kind of dark, and there were two oblivious hotel guests going at it in the pool. They were not just making out; they were naked and doing it. We just went about our catering business as they went about their monkey business. They didn't even notice us.

When they were done, I went over and offered them a cigarette.

Okay, not really. Really, I said, "Get a room." (I mean the pool was at a freaking hotel.)

Actually, I didn't go over at all. The captain finally went over (That's why he gets the big bucks) and said something. I think he surprised them; they were so involved in their activities that they thought they were alone.

Lost

Before navigators like Thomas Guides, Google Maps, MapQuest, and Waze were used in cars, way back in the 1990s, I was once driving from Long Island to Connecticut to a catering event and had the sheet of paper with my directions on it laying on the passenger seat beside me. As I drove down the highway with the windows rolled down on a beautiful sunny day, the paper flew out the window. Now I had no address.

I pulled over to a payphone (this was 1990 B.C., before cellphones) and called the emergency line of the company I was working for. I got a machine. I left a message. Waited about half an hour, called again, and got a machine again. I left a message explaining I had no idea how to get to the event, that the paper flew out the window (which sounds like an even worse excuse than the dog ate my homework, I know). After another half hour, I just drove home. I finally got a call back several hours later. They could not really be mad at me because they didn't pick up the phone for like two hours, and I was calling their emergency line.

Thank god for GPS and the other digital navigators that exist now. Otherwise, I would get lost every day.

God asked me if I wanted a sense of humor or sense of direction. I said, "A sense of humor." He gave me neither.

Chicken Tartar in a Basket

I worked for a caterer on Long Island for quite a while. One event was for a picnic outside and there were baskets of fried chicken put on each table. About halfway through the event, one of the servers discovered that some of the chicken was not cooked all the way through. I think he was going to eat a piece and noticed it. It was when we cleared the baskets after everyone was done, so oops, too late to do anything.

None of the guests complained and I checked all hospitals the next day to make sure no one got food poisoning. I'm kidding.

Anyway, I'm sure the chicken tartar diet is a great way to lose weight. The pounds just come off I've heard.

Falsely Accused

I worked for a staffing agency in New York and we were sent to work for a caterer, don't remember who it was at this point. The following week, the agency said they had a complaint about me: that I had been eating for much of the event.

I was baffled. I barely ate at the event except for a quick staff meal. I told him it wasn't me, but they kept insisting it was. So, I went down to the caterer's office, walked in, and there was a guy sitting at the desk. I told him I had worked an event for them, and I was being accused of eating a lot during the event. He looks at me and he says, "You're not the guy."

I said, "I know that! Please clear this up with the agency I work for." I wasn't sure if someone was caught eating a lot and gave my name, or there was just a mix up, but I didn't like being accused of doing something I didn't do.

I don't like being accused of things I do either. I prefer to get away with it.

Mono and Catering Don't Mix Well

When I was thirty years old, I got mono. (Yeah, I know. Most people get it in high school.) It was not fun. I was so tired.

I didn't work for about six weeks while I rested at my parent's house, then I slowly got back into it. I remember someone complained that I wasn't pulling my weight (I only weighed 165 pounds) and I said, "I just got over mono, you idiot."

They were like, "Oh sorry." Some people are clueless.

Dream

I had a dream once where I was out on the floor of an event and I looked down and I had bare feet. I was like, *Where did my shoes go?* I ran quickly away from the guests so no one would see. I went in the kitchen, found my shoes, put them on, and went back out to the party.

The captain of the event came up to me and asked, "Where are your shoes?" I looked down and again I was in bare feet. I was totally perplexed. I said to the captain, "I just put them on. I don't know what happened to them." I was so upset.

At least the shoes weren't Pradas. Those would have been expensive to lose. And at least it wasn't the dream where I'm in my underwear in public, so there's that.

It's always so funny to me how important shoes are to the caterers. They have to be shiny black—because if they are not, the guests won't have a good time?

Earthquake

I live in California, so there is a chance an earthquake could happen while an event is going on. A very small one did. While I was at the urinal in the bathroom. I was doing my thing and another butler, Brett Glazer, was standing at the stall next to me, and suddenly, I felt as if the floor was being raised up.

I look over at Brett, not sure if it was a tremor, and he says, "Yup, earthquake." What was funny to me was that he had not said a word all day to save his voice for a singing job the next day, so he had been writing everything down that he needed to say. The little 4.5 quake forced him to speak.

Coronavirus Killed Catering

In March 2020, I was still doing some catering on the side in between shooting my movies and doing a book tour for my book *Rainbow Relatives.* Again, the flexibility of doing catering is the greatest perk. Well, no one saw this coming. Well, maybe Nostradamus did back in 1566. Careful what you wish for, like thinking, *I don't want to do catering anymore.*

In early 2020, the biggest pandemic since 1918 took the world by storm. Coronavirus changed everything and it seemed to come out of nowhere. I was scheduled for quite a few jobs in March, and the news was getting worse and worse about this horrible virus that had shut down all of Italy and other countries. Events started getting canceled kind of a "just in case," and then everything was getting canceled. I worked a couple days at Netflix in the first week of March 2020. The cafeteria at Netflix enacted service where the employees could not touch the food on the buffet, and we had to hand it to them with tongs and wearing gloves. It was before the masks were required. I was supposed to work there quite a few times that month, but everything got closed down and most people were told to work from home.

Then all of California was on quarantine and lockdown, along with NYC, which got hit the worst. As of September, almost everything was still shut down and there was little to no acting or catering work.

My friend Matilda Szydagis was getting ready to play Zelda the Maid for a fourth season on *The Marvelous Mrs. Maisel* when everything stopped. These were her thoughts about the catering industry at the time. "Given the state of the world right now, who knows when catering will be available again in the future as a real means of income, if at all, until we get a vaccine and people everywhere start legit WEARING MASKS. Everyone needs to take this seriously and be responsible for themselves and respectful to others, which one would hope would automatically happen in a civilized society."

All events were canceled. Restaurants and bars closed. Everyone was affected by this. Weddings were canceled or postponed, which was a silver lining for those with cold feet.

In all of my fifty-six years of living (which is hard to do since I'm only forty), I have never seen a crisis this bad. As I'm writing this, it is now getting closer to the end of 2020 and no end in sight, we have no idea how much longer this will go on. California is spiking in cases.

I'm reminded of one year when I was supposed to work the Oscars, but I got a really bad flu that year and I had to cancel. That company did not like if you didn't work the Oscars. In fact, they used to say if you didn't work the Oscars, you couldn't work for them at all. We later found out they couldn't even legally do that.

NINETEEN

OTHER COOL AND CRAZY PEOPLE I WORKED WITH AND OTHER LOCATIONS

Let's face it. Everyone, no matter where they work, probably has a few crazy people that work with them and catering brings out some real loonies. Most are the fun kind of crazy, but there are also a few wackos.

The First "Me Too" Movement

There was a woman who catered for the same company I did around 2006, before the official "Me Too" movement—in fact, I think she tried to start it. She was a little touched, but not by her coworkers. Just in her head. She accused about ten different guys of sexual harassment, four of whom were gay. Maybe she believed they really did come on to her or harass her. Who knows? And I understand that most women who claim they've been attacked, assaulted, harassed, or abused, have been. But not all, and not this one.

The office at our catering company took her complaints seriously and began an investigation—as WELL they should. They called in the falsely accused men to question them. Very soon, it became clear that she was the problem, but for legal reasons they had to be very careful. It would still look bad if they let her go or fired her.

One time, this woman gave the finger to a coworker on the floor with guests around. When management heard I had seen her doing this, the supervisor came over and asked me, "Did you really see her do that? Would you testify to that?" They really wanted to find a legit reason to get rid of her.

The woman also happened to be Asian, so when someone was yelling at someone else to hurry up, saying, "Chop, chop," she thought they were talking to her, and she was very offended. She was definitely paranoid.

I got along with her fine, and I think she may have really thought these guys were doing what she said they had, but they weren't. I don't think they were trying to screw her. I suspect she had a screw loose.

Kim Kadel's Crazy Catering Memories

Kim is another person I catered with who remains a good friend. I worked many events with her back in the day. Kim taught me the expression "Shut your pie hole" about twenty years ago. I had never heard it before that, but I have heard it quite a bit since then. To this day, I still use it once in a while especially when someone honks their horn. So, I owe her a debt of gratitude for giving me that terrific expression to use in certain scenarios.

One of the events I did with Kim was at Radio City Music Hall, a party for everyone who had ever been on the cover of *Time* magazine up until that point, which was around 2000. Some folks who made the cover and were there were Tom Cruise and Nicole Kidman (who were married at the time), Muhammed Ali, and anyone else who was anyone, really. The event was staffed by Sterling Affair and Kim got me on the job. She still does some work for them and was currently their director of operations in 2020 during the coronavirus nightmare. While most caterers were totally closed down, their company helped serve 8,000 meals a week at New York Presbyterian Hospital at Columbia. I also worked with Kim for another caterer. We reminisced about a few stories when I called her in New York from California.

Here is one of our funny memories. I call it "F.U."

Kim and I had one of our biggest laughs driving to an event from NYC to New Jersey. There were four or five of us in the car. Kim and I were in the back seat, and the driver and a passenger in the front. We were going down this narrow, small road and there was traffic. A bicyclist with spandex on and a helmet was riding on the same road. Traffic was so slow that he kept passing us on the left, then we would catch up to him. Kim decided to do a backseat prank where she put her arm around the driver's seat and stuck her middle finger up near the window where the driver couldn't see it but the guy on the bike could. The biker kept looking over as it looked like the driver was flipping him off, giving him the finger. Meanwhile, the driver was looking straight ahead, totally oblivious and the guy on the bike was getting more and more angry at this driver who is not even looking at him, yet seemingly giving him the finger.

Kim and I were laughing in the backseat, being the immature people we were, and suddenly the guy on the bike pulled up next to the driver and yelled out really loudly, "F*&k you," which made Kim and I laugh even louder. The rest of the ride we just kept saying, "F#@* you" the way he did, and years later we still do it and bust out laughing.

Captains, Oh My Captains

As you know by now, they have what they call *captains* on catering jobs—but these individuals aren't the kind that go down with the ship. Captains are ones in charge of the events. They designate all the assignments, oversee everything, and they deal with the clients, which was a deal breaker for me regarding my decision to not ever captain.

Some captains are good, and some are on all-mighty power trips. And sometimes there is more than one captain, and they are not always on the same page. They might not even be in the same book. Sometimes one captain says, "Do this," while the other captain says, "Do that." Their goal seems to be to communicate as little as possible, so there ends up being a mix-up or a task is done wrong.

Sometimes I think that the prerequisite for being a captain is to be ANAL, condescending, and neurotic. Most companies definitely want those who pay strict attention to detail.

Some captains are honest, and some captains steal tips. I believe there is a special place down below for those who do the latter.

As I mentioned, I never wanted to be a captain because I didn't want to deal with the people in the catering office, some of the clients, or some of the butlers. I felt the stress was not worth the extra pay. The captains are not on top of the totem pole. That, in fact, would be the supervisors or salespeople who got the client.

Some captains treat the staff well and some are godawful people.

Then there are the "off-duty captains." I believe Marie Todd came up with this expression. These are butlers who are not captains but think they are—meaning, they think they can tell you what to do.

Good Captains

Anne Marie and the Cookie Abomination

Anne Marie Osgood was one of my favorite captains, and we shared many laughs together, including over the following story. We had snacks set out on a table for the client, including chocolate chip cookies. We are talking BIG cookies. HUGE! You could probably feed two people with half of one. Anyway, a guest came up and was fuming. He said to Anne Marie, "These cookies are way too big. They are an abomination."

At first, Anne Marie and I thought he was kidding. I mean, who calls a cookie an *abomination?* Turns out he wasn't kidding. He was so mad about it. I guess he thought dough was going to waste, that they were too big to eat. The chip on his shoulder was bigger than the chocolate chips in the humongous cookies. We laughed about it for a long time.

I was in New York a couple years after this in a bakery that had a stack of these really big cookies in their display, so I took a picture and sent it to her with the caption: "Abomination."

Anne Marie was one of the honest captains. She has a great story about an event she did, at a house party. I didn't work it, but those who did all got their $100 tip for the event in a check by the night of the event. Anne Marie was given one check for $700 by the host for the whole staff. Rather than have them wait for her to send their tip, she paid them out of pocket that night with her own personal checks.

Then, the next day, she lost the $700 check.

She had gone to the doctor in the morning, then ran errands, then went to the bank. She then realized the check was nowhere to be found. She knew she had it earlier in the day. She retraced her steps drove to all the places she had been. She got to the doctor's office and parked far from where she originally was. Somehow she saw the check in the middle of the road. This was a very windy day, mind you, so she was very lucky to find that check—really it was a miracle she found it—and I think she had to dodge a few cars going by to retrieve it.

Fran Ferrara

Francesca Ferrara was an excellent captain, who later did the booking out of the office and she was great there too. She was patient and always willing to work around scheduling conflicts. She is also a talented actress. She was a guest star on the finale of the show *Mad Men*. She was also on other shows like *Ugly Betty* and *Grey's Anatomy*. She was in a version of the play *As Is* in Hollywood and was excellent in it. She was one of my favorite people at any catering company.

David Applegate

David was a very good captain because he really knew what he was doing. Very professional. Strict without being a dick. He was known for making sure we had all our uniforms correct, and that we had our lighter, wine opener, and a pen, which were all part of the uniform. On some late-night shifts, some staff would be cut earlier than others if they wanted, but only if they had those items on them.

Vincent Braccia

Vinnie is the president of Top Shelf Staffing. Really a nice guy. I worked with him in NY about thirty years ago and then he started his own company.

....

A few more decent captains that pop up in my mind that I worked with were Doug Tompos (also a talented actor), Aaron Williams, Jen Balzer, Kim Mix, Emily King, Tony Filippone, Corrine and Brett Glazer, Rebecca and Rachel Short, Michael Albala, Steve Roman, and Enrique Martinez, Rosemary Larrazabal, Kathy Byron, Tony Raynor, Juan Monsalvez, Suna Bilsted, who was half Turkish like me, and Sophie Sharkov, among others. I am lucky to have worked with so many cool people.

Detach

Marie Todd, a dear friend with whom I've worked with for many years, taught me a trick for getting through the events and making the time go faster. I can always count on her to help me have a more pleasant experience when we work together. Marie taught me how to keep my sanity intact while working through a cocktail hour, or the whole event, whether it be chaotic or boring. She does what she calls *detaching* or *creative visualization* to establish a veil of protection around her. This comes in handy at events that are out of control when guests are unruly and rude. You just imagine that you are somewhere else, like in a science-fiction scenario, and pretend the catering event is not really real.

This could work at any job or in any situation you don't want to be in, I suppose. Marie also taught me what she calls the *Orange Cone Solution.* You imagine there are those orange construction cones around you, so the guests can't get to you. They need to stay back. I suppose this also could be called *zoning out.* Whatever you call it, it usually works.

Other Cool Locations I've Worked

Location, location, location.

That's a common phrase heard in real estate. In catering, we work in many different locations. All over. I've worked pretty much everywhere including offices, homes, parks, stadiums, clubs, and more. I worked in many a temple, and it's caused many a headache in my temples.

Here are a few of the more interesting places where I often worked.

Liberty Science Center: Jersey City, New Jersey

In the 1990s, I worked at the Liberty Science Center with my good friends Cara and Everett Chavez. It was a cool kind of museum. We'd have to drive all the way from Long Island to New Jersey—about an hour and a half drive right in the middle of rush hour—and we had to take a bridge or a tunnel and there were tolls, so we would carpool. It was actually a pretty cool place to work. It was mostly these corporate events and we would just pass food around. There was this one exhibit/display of these giant Madagascar cockroaches that had numbers on their back, and they would have them race against each other. They would open up a banana, then set the cockroaches down, and they were off and running toward it. It was fun to taunt them in the glass cage where they couldn't get to the food. I hate cockroaches.

Vendors would sometimes be at the events and would give out free samples to the guests. Cara remembers one of the vendors was selling a fancy dog food, and this lady, who was a guest at the event, said, with her very thick New York, Cindy Lauper-like accent, "But ya don't undastand. My dawg, she's a vegetarian!" (Like the dog decided to be a vegetarian.) This was like thirty years ago when even fewer **people** were vegetarians.

Rose Bowl: Pasadena, California

The best thing about working at the Rose Bowl were the concerts, although we really didn't get to see most of them anyway. Some performers who were there when I worked were: Ed Sheeran, Kenny Chesney, Jason Aldean, and Beyoncé and Jay Z.

These were very long shifts, like ten and a half hours, and the caterer would have sandwiches and chips for us when we first got there, and give us a half hour break five minutes after we clocked in. Then we would be working like nine hours without a break.

The worst thing was parking there—a nightmare—so far away from where we were working the event. If you got done with your shift before the concert ended it was fine, but if you got out at the same time as the concert goers, you were stuck in the parking lot for an extra hour that you did not get paid for.

A Venue in Las Vegas, Nevada

This was the furthest I drove and worked from where I lived, and I did it just once. I was not in California very long and needed work, so I took a job where we drove to Las Vegas for an event. They put the crew up for a night in a hotel and we drove back the next day. Somehow I got stuck driving two or three strangers in my car. Had I known, I would have brought more CDs with me because they wanted to listen to some music on the way there, but I had such an odd collection in my car at the time that I knew I was in the minority of liking them. I did have Linda Ronstadt's first greatest hits CD, and everyone liked that.

It was a five-hour drive. I think we went to the casino while there, and I probably lost the money I made at the event in the slots. I was paid extra for gas money, but I don't think the catering company paid us for our drive time. I didn't know any better back then.

Since this event was in Vegas and what happens in Vegas stays in Vegas, I can't tell you about the actual event. Actually, I don't even remember the event, just the horrible drive there and back.

Griffith Park Observatory: Los Angeles, California

The view from the location of this event space is beautiful, the building is high up so you can see most of L.A.. There is a planetarium there, although I have never been in it.

The Conga Room: Downtown L.A.

The Conga Room is a part of the L.A. Live entertainment complex. It's a place where the music is so loud you need earplugs in your ears. I think maybe they own stock in hearing aids. My best day at the Conga Room was when we got paid to do nothing. We arrived and were told the event had been cancelled at the last minute. If this happens, they still have to pay you for four hours. If it's less than twenty-four hours' notice, they have to pay you for two hours.

The American Museum of Natural History: New York, New York

I worked many events at the Natural History Museum in NYC many years ago, which was kinda cool. I enjoyed seeing the displays of all the animals and cavemen. Guests were eating beef next to a life-size, stuffed prehistoric bison.

The Pacific Design Center: West Hollywood, California

One of the waiters I know calls PDC the "Pacific *Disaster* Center." The worst part of that place for me was moving and rearranging heavy furniture before and after an event. It was in West Hollywood, where parking is impossible to find. But it was one of the few places we didn't have to pay for our parking.

The GRAMMY Museum: Los Angeles, California

I love music, so working there was fun for me. It was kinda cool seeing the displays, and we usually just passed food around.

TWENTY

GIVE CATERERS THE RESPECT THEY DESERVE

I want to close with suggesting—and by *suggesting,* I mean "strongly insisting," —that you be kind to the caterers when you go to an event. Now, if a server has a really bad attitude or is doing a terrible job that doesn't mean you have to ignore it, but let's assume that 95 percent of the catering team will be working very hard to ensure you have a good time and enjoy the event you are attending. They work hard to make sure your event goes well. They work long hours and they work late hours.

Tip the Staff

Tip generously, especially if you live in a home worth millions and you and your guests all just got excellent service.

Leo Penza was once a captain on a job many years ago where we worked very hard. The host didn't hire enough staff and there was so much special service to be done, it was just nonstop. We served a several-course meal with demanding guests. When Leo went to get our money, the guy gave the exact amount. No tip. So, Leo stood there calmly and asked, "Was everything okay? Was the service okay? Because my crew worked really hard," or something like that. I wasn't standing there to hear the conversation, but the guy finally gave Leo like a $10 tip to give to each of us. Better than nothing. Good for Leo for standing up for his staff.

I used to work with Leo and his wife Lily on quite a few events in the 1990s and also Lily's sister, Haydee Feliciano, who is one of my best friends to this day.

Second Amendment of Catering: The Right to Bear Cell Phones

I will not give up my cell phone at an event. They would have to pry it from my cold dead hands. I will never use it on the floor or have it in sight, but I do need to have it with me because I can lose acting job offers or catering offers from other companies if they call and I don't get back to them promptly. Caterers are very strict about cell phones. They will threaten to send you home if they see yours out. I'm smart enough not to have it out but some workers are just plain stupid and have them out on the floor in front of guests while they are working. Only a handful, but a few bad apples (or Apple phones, in this case) in sight can ruin it for the rest.

Since most butlers and waiters are actors, they NEED their cell phones. Texts and emails come in frequently with notices of possible work, and if you don't respond within as few as ten or fifteen minutes, your chance to audition or accept a role may be lost. For example, alerts come in from L.A. Casting to submit for certain projects or a casting company may text or email saying they have work for the next day. If you don't respond quickly, tough luck.

As long as we are discreet with checking our phones, it should not be a problem.

Once I was working a catering job behind a buffet on a Sunday evening. It was almost 7PM and guests were about to arrive. My cell phone was buzzing. I ducked down under the buffet and answered. It was a casting company asking if I was available the next day for background work on a commercial for McDonald's: a two spot, which meant double pay. I said, "Yes, I'm available," and the next day I made over $700. Had I not answered the phone call right away, I would have lost out on that. Mind you, it was a Sunday night at almost 7PM when the call came in, a time when one might not expect to get a work call, but these calls truly may come in at any time.

I could be doing laps in a pool for half hour and miss out.

Meanwhile, you might not get a call for months, so you don't want to miss the few that do come in.

At one catering event for which I was booked, I arrived to work at the Dolby Theatre. When we got there, they told us we had to give our phones up for five hours during the event. I said I couldn't do that since I could lose money from possible jobs offers so I needed my phone on me. Someone else also complained that they should have told us that in advance, not when we got to the event. The guy in charge said that if I wanted, they could sign me out and I would still get paid two hours. I said that's fine. So, I got paid two hours work and I was there for only five minutes.

Sometimes, we worked at locations like houses in the hills where reception is horrible, so I'm sure I've lost some work that way.

Funny story. A guy I worked with quite a few years back had to use his phone, so he snuck off to the restroom and into the stall. When he left the stall, one of the owners of the company was at the sink and saw the waiter walk out without washing his hands. (This was pre-coronavirus). The owner complained to the captain. The waiter explained that he didn't actually do #1 or #2. He just had to check his phone for business.

Stealing Tips

To reiterate, there are some caterers who steal tips. They charge the client and then don't give it to their workers. The biggest disrespect to catering staff is the keeping of their tips. At an event for which I was not present, the client asked the captain, if she were to send the tip to the caterer will they get it? He was honest and said, "No," so I think she gave it directly to him.

The next day he got a call from the caterer. They wanted him to come into the office. He knew the client must have said something, so he just said, "I know what it's about and I won't be coming into the office and I won't be working for you anymore," or something like that.

I told my mom years ago how caterers often keep the tips, so when my sister got married my mom told the caterer she wanted to give the staff their tips directly. The caterer would not allow it and insisted on putting it on the bill. I'm betting the staff probably did not see it.

A Good "Christian" Captain

I worked at the event space, which I will call "Freebell." They have many events there, and it was also a theatre. After I no longer worked for them, my partner did, and he actually got stiffed by a captain I will call "Vanessa Cortez" with whom we had worked many times. Vanessa claimed to be a Christian woman. I only say this because it's the fake ones who taint the good ones. So, for her to steal tips from the people working for her is UN-Christian-like. Plus, she used to be a butler before she was a captain, so she knows what it's like to have your tips get stolen.

My partner Carlos worked an event during Christmas time at Freebell, and the client came up to him towards the end and asked, "Who do I give this to, to give to the staff?" She had an envelope that obviously had cash for tips in it. Carlos directed her to see Vanessa. Vanessa did give $100 of it to the bartender and to the chef. Nothing was given to the other three workers, including Carlos.

The bartender asked Carlos "Hey, did you get your tip?"

Carlos said, "No, I'll see if she gives it a little later." Carlos waited a few days to see if Vanessa would give the rest of the crew their tips. None came. So, he outright asked her, "Was there a tip? She said, "No."

Carlos knew the name of the client, so I volunteered to call the client for him. I told her, "A friend of mine had worked the Christmas event, and it was awkward of me to ask, but was the envelope you gave to Vanessa supposed to go to all the workers?"

The client said, "Yes, of course, they all should have gotten some." I then sent an email directly to the Vanessa, telling her we knew there was a tip for the event, and she should have given it to her staff. How dare she steal their tips! This was the email I sent to Vanessa:

Hello, Vanessa,

I am writing on behalf of Carlos, regarding the Freebell event on November 19 for the REDACTED. Carlos was a little worried about pursuing this matter even though he is entitled to, for obvious reasons. First of all, I have PROOF that you took tip money that was supposed to go to the three waiters at an event for the REDACTED. SOLID proof, so there is no need to deny or make excuses. Thou shalt not steal, I know, you know this expression. There is another "Christian" value, forgiveness, which I'm sure Carlos will do and this whole matter will be put behind if the three servers are paid the $100 each, they are owed. And this is what you need to do now, to make it right. Everyone makes mistakes, Vanessa, you now have the chance to correct that mistake and learn from it. Carlos sent you an email and gave you a chance to rectify the situation right when it happened. You lied and said only the bartender, you, and the chef, and the musicians were tipped and not the three servers, which in itself sounds suspicious enough.

I have investigated in the last few weeks and know for a fact that money was given ***for each*** *server (musicians were separate and taken care of, this is a fact). You must give the servers what is rightfully theirs. They worked hard for it, and you had no right to take it. I would expect this from someone like Morey Seamstress, not from you.*

So, all you have to do, is give them their money and the subject will never come up again.

HOWEVER: *If you choose to continue to deny it and lie, then I will go with Carlos, to Human Resources and the president of Freebell, and to the other servers that worked that day, and tell them what you did. I'm not bluffing here; I have* ***proof*** *and it's a fact you did it. But I really don't want to do that. I really don't want to get you in trouble. This is not about being vengeful.*

I truly hope you will do the right "Christian," moral thing here. And everyone will forgive you for your momentary lack of judgment. I will assume this would not affect how much Carlos works in the future for Freebell, or that could cause a problem with HR as well. I also assume you will ***never again*** *take tip money that is owed to your hard-working staff (There is strong evidence that some servers have not gotten tips owed to them in the past, for several events).Vanessa, you are better than this, please do the right thing.*

Rick Karatas

She didn't respond, instead she showed the email to the General Manager. Carlos was then called into the office, they did a "fake investigation" and said there was a misunderstanding and that they all would receive $50 (it was supposed to be $100). Carlos was given a written warning for contacting the client. Technically, the staff should never call a client directly, but you know what? If I were the client, I would want to know that a captain is keeping the staff's tips. The company Freebell was protecting Vanessa.

Shame on them and shame on her, a so-called Christian stealing tips near Christmas.

Party Down

Okay, so if you watched this show you might not think caterers deserve respect by the way this staff acts on this show. I didn't watch the TV show *Party Down* when it came out. When I started writing this book, I figured I would watch it, since it is related to the topic of my book. I also love the actress Jane Lynch, who is in it. Funny show, though extremely unrealistic.

For example, one scene showed a waiter eating nonchalantly behind the buffet with guests and people in charge around. Now, I'm not saying servers don't ever eat behind the buffet, but they do it discretely. There's a trick to it. You sneak something into a napkin, then duck down under the buffet as if you are grabbing something from underneath, like extra plates, plasticware, or napkins. Then you wolf it down and reappear with whatever "red herring" you are putting on the buffet.

You can also do the "turn your back" trick and stuff something in your mouth if there is a wall behind you.

The same goes when passing hors d' oeuvres. You don't eat them on the floor, you sneak them on your way back in the hallway before the kitchen. The trick is to save one if you are close to the kitchen. As you head toward the kitchen with that lone item, if a guest says, "Ooh, I'll take that" you just tell them, "Oh, this one fell on the floor." This works 90 percent of the time. A few will still take it.

Party Down had a great cast. In season 2, Megan Mullally from *Will and Grace* joined the cast. The amount of stuff this fictional crew gets away with is insane. Would never happen in real life—but it's TV. The one thing that stands out to me on the show is that they didn't have a kitchen staff at the events. The waiters would be plating up the food. It seemed like no one was cooking it, and there definitely wasn't enough staff for most of the events. (Okay, that last part is believable because some companies try to save money by understaffing.)

I actually did a day of background work as an actor on the show, in a fundraiser scene. I'm seen for .00001 seconds but it was a fun day.

Another Journal entry from 1998

I found this in an old journal:

I turned down catering work for tomorrow night to go to a class where agents and casting directors come. Priorities. It will pay off in the long run.

Man, I was so naïve back then, hahaha. Actually, this showed that I had enough respect for myself to take my acting career seriously and try not to let catering get in the way of career my goals. I wasn't always successful with this, sometimes catering did suck me in.

Rude Guests

Another event Cara Chavez remembers was when a couple had a party for their four-year-old, which was really a party to show off their new Bentley. They hired a sushi chef to shuck oysters. A train went around the house that the kids could ride on. Expensive birthday for a four-year-old. A particular guest was very rude to Cara that day. The guest demanded that Cara go get her child some shrimp, and when Cara brought it over, the woman screamed, "How dare you bring that over like that?! You go over there and cut it up!"

Cara walked by me and said, "I'm done, I'm about to clock that lady."

I said, "Cara, calm down, go take a break, relax, chill, take a valium, like a normal person." That's a line in the movie *Desperately Seeking Susan* that my dad used to quote a lot.

Anyway, rude guests are like cockroaches. We just want them to go away.

Speaking of cockroaches, Cara told me that when we used to work weddings at a temple in Long Island, they would always bring out the same fake wedding cake for show. They would then wheel it back to the kitchen and cut up the real cake and bring it out on plates. She said the fake cake was never cleaned and there would be roaches crawling all over it.

Class-Action Lawsuits

One company I worked for had absolutely no respect for their staff. Over the years, at least four class action lawsuits were brought against them and I got four checks out of the settlements. One was for $2,800. One for about $500, one $1,200. They just didn't care. They would rather rip us off any way they could and pay a few fines.

Advice to Those Who Want to Get into Catering

Here's my advice (and some from my friends).

- Don't do it if you are not a glutton for punishment
- Don't do it if you are looking to lose weight
- Don't do it if you don't have patience
- Don't do it if you are not a people person
- Don't do it if you *are* a people person
- From Chef Marcos Rodriguez: *"DON'T! Just kidding. I'd say that it's a really good industry to be in if you like working in new places at any given time. You could be working anywhere from a gigantic, beautiful home*

with a great view to the back alley of an old theater for a movie premier. It can be such a great experience to be working with menus different from one day to another, one event to another. I would also advise them to know your life is dictated by you, and not to you or for you."

- Remember, "It's just food." Sometimes these caterers or clients act like lives are in danger or something.
- From Chef Keith Johnson: *"Make sure it's what you love to do and find a niche that makes you happy. Don't just settle. It's a give-100-percent kind of job."*
- Have Tums or Alka-Seltzer on hand at all times for upset stomachs.
- Buy very, very, very, very comfortable shoes.
- Don't drink the water.
- *"NEVER YELL AT A MURDERER."* This advice comes from Krysta Florczyk, who worked an awards show at the L.A. Live Event Deck. She scolded rappers who just got off the stage and were going through pastries. They started putting their hands in the pastry that was plated to go out, and Krysta yelled, "Hey what are you doing?" A houseman later told her that the guy she yelled at had once been convicted of murder and she probably should keep her mouth shut. Another time, she thought someone was going to come back and shoot her. He'd put his face in a dessert and security had to physically escort him out. He was gonna come after her and hurt her.

- Don't be vindictive: A guy I work with was punished by a supervisor once when his cousin, whom he had referred for the job, didn't show up. The supervisor gave him the four tables his cousin would have been bussing on top of the four tables he was given, instead of just dividing the tables up among the other staff. He was just mean. In the words of Taylor Swift, "Why Ya Gotta Be So Mean?"
- Don't show up to work with a hickey or two. (Don't ask me how I know this one.)

Sudi-isms

These are expressions I have come up with while catering.

- "I gave my two-week notice two YEARS ago."
- "Thank god, my writing and acting career is taking off soon."
- "I have low tolerance for high-maintenance people."
- "Does this tie make me look fat?"
- "I don't like my tone, I'm leaving." (I said this a lot when I catered.)
- "I hate to see food go to waste when there are people starving (pause) . . . in my apartment."
- "Too many chiefs on too much opium." (When captains gave conflicting orders.)
- "You only live once, unless you are Shirley MacLaine." (I said this to a guest at an event once and a few minutes later I saw Shirley MacLaine as a guest there.)

A Few Popular Catering Expressions

Here are a few expressions you might hear a lot.

- *"It's not catering unless you do it at least three times."* This is one of the most common expressions in the catering world. You can set up a whole buffet a certain way, then the party planner or captain or client decide they want it a different way after you did all the work. God forbid they get there early enough to decide what they want. "Place a table in that corner," "No wait put it in this corner," "On third thought, put it back where it originally was." "Fold the napkins this way, no fold them that way even though you already folded most of them." Argggghhhh.
- *"Can I go home now?"* I usually said this fifteen minutes into a shift.
- *"There's no crying in cooking."* (Chef Keith Johnson)
- *"We're saving lives."* Some people take catering way too seriously.
- *"Never tell the client no, even if that's the answer."* Instead say, "Let me check," and then don't return to the table.

In Closing

I hope you have enjoyed these stories and learned a thing or two about the catering world. I had fun writing it, and as much as I joke, catering is not a bad job to do, depending on who you are working for.

You are making sure people have a good time at an event and seeing that they get plenty of food and drink. And even when I did not want to be working, I always gave good service to the guests. I worked with so many wonderful people over the years, some of whom I've mentioned, but many I lost touch with and hope they are doing well.

Thanks again everyone, for reading about my experiences, and remember, my book is like potato chips. You can't have just one. (Last food pun in the book, I promise.) So, feel free to get one for someone else.

Chow.

Pasta la vista, baby.

Okay, THAT was the last pun.

ACKNOWLEDGEMENTS

Throughout the book, I have mentioned many wonderful people I worked with over the years. Individuals that I didn't mention before, I will here, like Gary Livingood, who used to hire staff for L.A. events (he's now in real estate); the lovely Andrea Giardino in NYC, for whom I worked many catering events; Robert Swingle, whom I catered for in NYC; Stuart Shultz at Perfect Pear Caterers in NYC; and Boyz in the Kitchen in Burbank, California.

Some other friends I've worked with or for over the years and want to give a shout out to (as opposed to ones I want to shout at) include Jon Brothers, Tom Treadwell, Mike Ramon, Karen Jefferson, Pim Hendrix, Pamela Evans, Michael Vitiello Pamela Ademic, Jabari Jones and Carlos Antonio (who were both in my movie), Eddie Martinez, Marti Hendricks, Aaron Williams, Rob Findlay (in some of my sketches and a great Elvis impersonator), Melissa Klein, a great singer, and Lori Mathews who did payroll—very nice and obviously she is important as she helped me get paid!

Thank you to my editor, Stephanie Gunning. A special thanks to Frank Hinterberger, for doing some editing and fact checking for me at an early stage in the process.

I am grateful to Carlos Romani for all he does for me, including helping take pictures for the Facebook page "How Catering Sucked the Life Right Out of Me," and the cover of this book, and for being supportive of my creative endeavors.

RESOURCES

Please come visit me on my website. That's where you can find news about my writing, acting, and producing projects.

sudirick.com

Watch my movie, *Walk a Mile in My Pradas,* on Amazon Prime.

Websites of People and Businesses Mentioned in the Book

Serves You Right Catering
https://www.servesyourightcaters.com

The Raging Skillet
https://www.theragingskillet.com

Natalie Sofer Weddings and Events
https://www.nataliesoferweddingsandevents.com

Wok Star Cater
https://wokstarcatering.com

Corrine's Concepts in Catering
http://www.corinnescatering.com

Demetra George
http://www.demetrageorge.net/about
Dr. Ira Sacker

http://www.sackermd.com/about_sacker_center_biographies_dr_ira_sacker.asp

The Laurel Foundation
https://www.laurel-foundation.org

Matilda Szydagis
www.matildaszydagis.com

Levi Kreis
https://www.levikreis.com

Top Shelf Staffing
https://www.topshelfstaffers.com

Mitch Hara and Jason Stuart show
https://www.smotheredTV.com

David Lee Photography
https://davidaleephotography.com

Sterling Affair
https://sterlingaffair.com

ABOUT THE AUTHOR

SUDI "RICK" KARATAS grew up in Syosset, New York, and now resides in Van Nuys, California. As a Gemini, he goes by two names. He's the author of *Rainbow Relatives: Real World Stories and Advice on How to Talk to Kids About LGBTQ Families and Friends* and the writer and producer of the film *Walk a Mile in My Pradas.* He's written many screenplays and songs and wrote a letter to Dear Abby once. For more info, go to www.sudirick.com.

Made in the USA
Coppell, TX
12 December 2020